Pilgrims on the Ohio

Pilgrims on the Ohio

THE RIVER JOURNEY & PHOTOGRAPHS OF REUBEN GOLD THWAITES, 1894

ESSAYS BY ROBERT L. REID AND DAN HUGHES FULLER

INDIANA HISTORICAL SOCIETY

INDIANAPOLIS 1997

The paper in this publication meets the minimum requirements of American National Standard for
Information Sciences—Permanence of Paper for Printed Library Materials, ANSI Z39.48–1984. ∞

Library of Congress Cataloging-in-Publication Data

Thwaites, Reuben Gold, 1853–1913.
    Pilgrims on the Ohio : the river journey & photographs of Reuben
Gold Thwaites, 1894 / essays by Robert L. Reid and Dan Hughes
Fuller.
       p.   cm.
    Includes excerpts from Thwaites' Afloat on the Ohio, originally
published in 1897.
    Includes bibliographical references.
    ISBN 0–87195–118–5
    1. Thwaites, Reuben Gold, 1853–1913—Journeys—Ohio River.
2. Ohio River—History—Pictorial works. 3. Ohio River—Description
and travel. 4. Ohio River—Social life and customs. I. Reid,
Robert L., 1938-   . II. Fuller, Dan Hughes.   III. Thwaites, Reuben
Gold, 1853–1913. Afloat on the Ohio. Selections.   IV. Title.
F519.T56   1997
977'.031—dc21   97-24067
                                             CIP

CONTENTS

The publication of this book is the latest stage in a journey that began in May 1894 in Brownsville, Pennsylvania. The journey started privately as a family's summer vacation and historical pilgrimage. It continued publicly with the publication of Reuben Gold Thwaites's book *Afloat on the Ohio*.

When Thwaites died suddenly in 1913 the river trip faded into the memories of his family members. Copies of his travel narrative languished on the back shelves of libraries. Meanwhile, the photographs that Thwaites took on the trip remained where they had been since 1894—in the family album.

The public rediscovery of the photographs began in 1986 when a grandson in California donated the album to the State Historical Society of Wisconsin. In 1991 Dr. Robert L. Reid visited the Society and selected several images for use on the *Always a River* exhibition barge that traveled the length of the Ohio River that summer. Next Dr. Reid organized, and Dan Fuller curated, an exhibition of the photographs called *Afloat on the Ohio, 1894*. Since 1995 thousands in Indiana, Ohio, Pennsylvania, and Illinois have seen this exhibition, and it continues to circulate at sites along the river that gave it birth.

Now, 103 years after the first oar was put in the water, the written account of the family's float down the Ohio River finally has been united with the pictures taken along the way. The publication of *Pilgrims on the Ohio: The River Journey & Photographs of Reuben Gold Thwaites* allows a new generation to travel the length of the Ohio River in a rowboat, sleep out under the stars, and meet the citizens of 1894.

The best journeys never end.

ACKNOWLEDGMENTS

This publication was made possible with the support of the State Historical Society of Wisconsin, the Indiana Humanities Council, and the Indiana Historical Society. A number of individuals have provided invaluable assistance. Our sincere appreciation goes to Peter T. Harstad, Thomas A. Mason, Paula Corpuz, Shirley S. McCord, Kathleen M. Breen, and J. Kent Calder at the Indiana Historical Society; Nicolette Bromberg at the State Historical Society of Wisconsin; Barbara Weaver Smith at the Indiana Humanities Council; John Streetman at the Evansville Museum of Arts and Science; and Charles Parrish at the U.S. Army Corps of Engineers, Louisville District. Thanks also to Rita Kohn, Christine Schelshorn, Jack and Sandy Custer, and Kenneth Gladish.

*O*n 11 June 1894 four travelers arrived at the con-
fluence of the Ohio and Mississippi Rivers. This place,
Cairo, Illinois, was their final destination, the termination
of a six-week adventure floating down the Ohio River in a fifteen-foot
rowboat. The four passengers were Reuben and Jessie Thwaites, their
ten-year-old son Fredrik, and Jessie's brother, William Daniel Turvill.
Starting at Brownsville, Pennsylvania, they traveled down the
Monongahela River to the place where it joins the Allegheny to form
the Ohio River. From this historic place at Pittsburgh, the Forks of the
Ohio, the family began its 981-mile trip down the main stem. In all,
the river sojourn took them nearly eleven hundred miles.

The propensity of Americans to travel is a well-known national
characteristic. By the 1890s railroads had opened up almost all parts of
the country to tourism, resulting in a substantial increase in mobility for
vacationing families. Travelers were encouraged to go west by rail to
see such spectacular settings as Yellowstone and Yosemite, the nation's
first nonurban parks. Most visitors to these wilderness areas were trans-
ported there by one of the nation's four transcontinental railroads in the
comfort of Pullman sleeping cars. Why did Reuben Gold Thwaites, a
historian employed as chief administrator of the State Historical Society
of Wisconsin and whose interest was in the "American West," opt to
take his family on a trip down the Ohio River in a rowboat?

Answers to this question are found in his narrative report. In 1897,
three years after their summer adventure, the story of the family's travel
was published in a book, *Afloat on the Ohio: An Historical Pilgrimage of a
Thousand Miles in a Skiff, from Redstone to Cairo.*[1] In his preface Thwaites
called the excursion a pleasure trip or "outing." From this perspective it
was a family vacation on the "Pilgrim," the boat used by the Thwaites
family to enjoy the many lakes near their home in Madison, Wisconsin.
Both the boat and its four passengers reached the starting point at
Brownsville and returned from Cairo via the nation's most efficient
form of transportation—the railroad. From Brownsville the travelers
floated downstream using oars, paddles, and even a sail to propel their
skiff. At night they found suitable camping places to pitch their two
small tents.

Recreation was not the only motive for the Ohio River pilgrimage.
Thwaites wrote that he was "quite as much interested in gathering 'local
color' for his studies of Western history as he was in cultivating a holi-
day tan." Noting the importance of the Ohio River in the development
of the West, he said, "I wished to know the great waterway intimately

in its various phases,—to see with my own eyes what the borderers saw; in imagination, to redress the pioneer stage, and repeople it."[2]

Thwaites's definition of western history was one which he shared with his close friend and colleague Frederick Jackson Turner. Thwaites wrote that "the story of the Ohio is the story of the West," and he dedicated *Afloat on the Ohio* to Turner, who was then a faculty member at the University of Wisconsin. The far west with its vast spaces, beautiful vistas, and unspoiled wilderness was attracting mounting public interest in the final decades of the nineteenth century. Turner's explanation for the course of American history, the "frontier thesis," coincided with a developing national anxiety about the closing of opportunity, which was heightened by labor unrest in the cities, agrarian radicalism in the countryside, and a major depression that began in 1893. But viewed from the perspective of place rather than process, it was the Old Northwest and the Ohio valley, later described as the "Old West," which captured the historical imaginations of both Turner and Thwaites.[3]

Throughout his narrative Thwaites makes it clear that the family considered travel to be an enriching educational experience. This attitude, shared by many well-to-do Americans, could have led the Thwaites family to return to England for another bicycle tour. The family also enjoyed canoeing, and Thwaites had traveled down the major rivers of Wisconsin and Illinois accompanied by his wife Jessie or his brother-in-law William. These earlier excursions had led to his first travel narrative, *Historic Waterways*, in 1888. A trip west to the Rocky Mountains or Pacific Coast would have been within their means, particularly since Thwaites had the support of the State Historical Society of Wisconsin for his six-week journey.[4] Ten years earlier Thwaites had visited New Mexico and Colorado as he considered founding a newspaper in the Southwest. He had invited a recent graduate of the University of Wisconsin, young Fred Turner, to join him in this publishing venture.

In reporting on this western trip for the *Wisconsin State Journal*, Thwaites gave ample expression to the clichés and stereotypes of his generation. He wrote that "only a keen desire for rapidly acquired wealth could induce a man of taste" to settle in Kansas City. In Tombstone, Arizona, he encountered cowboys whom he described as follows: "specimens of the animal lounge about upon every hand, with a fierce display of revolvers and rifles, a good deal of swagger, long-boots, spurs, gad whips, fringed buckskin breeches, and the widest possible sombreros." Commenting on the diversity of peoples in cosmopolitan Santa Fe, New Mexico, he wrote, "the white berating the

Mexican as a shiftless whelp, the Mexican characterizing the white as an avaricious shark." On his return he expressed his "taste" by making his next career move a position with the State Historical Society of Wisconsin. However, his trip in 1884 indicates clearly that Thwaites had firsthand experience with the trans-Mississippi West.[5]

After his graduation from Wisconsin, Turner taught in the history department before leaving for Johns Hopkins University to earn his Ph.D. Returning to Madison in 1889, he presented his ideas on the frontier to a national audience a few years later. In his famous address, "The Significance of the Frontier in American History," Turner argued that historians should direct their attention to the area where wilderness and civilization met in the New World.

The frontier thesis, replete with understanding about the movement of people through regions or sections that were once wilderness, continues to have an impact on what it means to be an American. These ideas took form in the reading room of the State Historical Society of Wisconsin, which Thwaites encouraged Turner and other young scholars to use. Turner taught his seminar classes in this room, where the rich collection of documents, newspapers, and records collected by Thwaites and his predecessor, Lyman C. Draper, were housed. Both Thwaites and Turner had strong roots in central Wisconsin, and it

Frederick Jackson Turner in his office at the State Historical Society of Wisconsin, ca. 1892

State Historical Society of Wisconsin WHi (X3) 35004

seemed natural that they would become colleagues. Turner was born and raised in Portage, while Thwaites had spent his teenage years near

Oshkosh. Shaped during their formative years by conditions close to the frontier experience, the two scholars centered their primary research interests on settings east of the Mississippi River.

The selection of the "Pilgrim" as the family's means of conveyance represented the same careful planning and deliberate choice as did the Ohio River. Throughout the nineteenth century a popular means of seeing the Ohio valley was to travel by steamboat. The Thwaites family members, however, were ardent canoeists and boaters, and they selected this mode of travel in order to experience more fully the historic sites along their chosen route.

To document his research Thwaites kept detailed notes that he recorded daily. Before leaving, he prepared a one-volume alphabetized pocket set of notes on the sites along the river. He filled three pocket-size diaries on the trip. Basically, *Afloat on the Ohio* is the "Log of the Pilgrim," a day-by-day travel narrative drawn from his notes. The book also may be seen as a preview of Thwaites's future historical work. In particular, it suggests the monumental editing of earlier travel writings that would characterize much of his scholarship. Considerably more than the story of a family's summer adventure, *Afloat on the Ohio* contains long narrative passages about the places and the historic personages associated with the sites the family visited. Extensive supple-

mentary material, including a twenty-four-page "Historical Outline of the Ohio Valley Settlement," an annotated "selected list" (forty-nine) of previous Ohio River travel accounts, and an index complete the book. His familiarity with Turner's ideas of the process of westward movement is clear. In his outline Thwaites moves through stages from backwoods pioneers to cattle raisers followed by agricultural settlers. Through bloody struggles with the Indians, he wrote, these backwoodsmen steadily "pushed back the rampart of savagery, and won the Ohio Valley for civilization."[6]

As a scholar Thwaites was receptive to developing theories and new forms of technology. In addition to his notes he documented the Ohio River journey with a small Kodak camera manufactured by George Eastman. Thwaites noted photographic occasions throughout the text of *Afloat on the Ohio* in several ways: "I clambered up to photograph [a log cabin or a farm house or a junk boat]"; "I took my snap-shot [of a family or a fleet of boats]"; and "I took a kodak . . . of a group of tousle-headed children." Thwaites observed that even the most impoverished shantyboaters were familiar with handheld cameras like the Kodak. The Kodak's introduction in 1888 caused a snapshot craze in which ordinary people had the ability to take their own pictures. For the first time amateurs began to produce more photographs than professionals. As Thwaites put it, "No child of nature is so simple in these days, as not to recognize a kodak."[7]

The initial success of the original Kodak camera brought forth a continuing pattern of improvement, and the introduction of new models became a standard feature of the Eastman company. New models provided regular occasions for promoting the snapshot camera through advertising. Thwaites took these photographs using a #2 Kodak purchased in 1891 for thirty-five dollars to provide the family with lasting memories of its trip. In doing so he was applying an advertising theme that George Eastman introduced with the #3, 4, and related model Kodaks: "Travellers and Tourists use it to obtain a picturesque diary of their travels." Thwaites's early use of the snapshot camera supports the observation of Susan Sontag that photography developed "in tandem with one of the most characteristic of modern activities: tourism."[8]

Yet another form of technological innovation accompanied the introduction of the inexpensive snapshot camera. To display the images, simple photograph albums were prepared. Earlier forms included elaborate, brass-framed, velvet-covered albums to present daguerreotypes and the carte de visite or visiting-card albums used by soldiers during the Civil War. Snapshot albums such as the Ohio River album were assembled from heavy paper stock and identified by hand-lettered covers. This format was used by Thwaites for other travels, including his earliest album that documented a summer bicycling excursion in England in 1891.

Such albums may be seen as a form of the "home mode" of visual communication. Amateur photographers were able to preserve the images and present them to a selected audience, almost always either family or close friends, in an orderly, systematic way. They were the result of a sequence that included planning the trip, taking the snapshots while traveling, developing the snapshots, editing and captioning the individual images, and exhibiting them to others.[9] This pattern, familiar to vacation goers today, had an added feature on the Ohio sojourn in that Thwaites was also using the camera as an aid to his memory. The photographs, with their careful captions including place and date, complemented his daily notes. Thus the visual images from the trip helped Thwaites recall the sense of place for scholarly uses in parallel fashion to his dual purpose of taking a family vacation and gathering local color for his writings on the developing American West.

None of the photographs were used as illustrations in *Afloat on the Ohio*, and there is no evidence to suggest that Thwaites had any interest in such an application. However, he did select several commercial photographs of Cincinnati to complement the second edition of his travel narrative when it was published in 1903. What is truly remarkable is that his Ohio River album, together with the original negatives, has been preserved. Two major reasons explain this: his meticulous care of personal effects, including letters, diaries, and albums, and the generosity of his descendants, who began donating his collection to the State Historical Society of Wisconsin in 1938. The result is an album of photographs taken in 1894 and intended for home viewing that provides us with a treasure of visual images displaying the Ohio River as it was more than one hundred years ago. Taken by a photographer whose preconceived notions of the river scenery was most likely limited to sketches in magazines such as *Harper's Weekly*, photographs shot in a round format serve both as historical documents and as images worthy of display for their surprisingly good artistic qualities.

Reuben Gold Thwaites was born 15 May 1853 in Dorchester, a suburb of Boston, Massachusetts. His parents were William George and Sarah Bibbs Thwaites who married in 1844 in England and immigrated to the United States in 1850. William was a cabinetmaker, and Sarah was from a family of substantial means. William and Sarah divorced in 1858, and little is known about the family until 1866 when Sarah and her three children moved to Omro, Wisconsin. The needs of a single-parent household influenced Thwaites's education. While he did not

graduate from high school, it is clear that he was an able and bright student. Thwaites worked on farms, taught school, became a reporter for the *Oshkosh Times*, and served as a stringer for major metropolitan newspapers. In 1874 he pursued graduate courses in economic history, international law, and literature at Yale. Once again Thwaites did not earn a degree. On his return to Wisconsin in 1876 he settled in Madison, where he worked as city editor and then as managing editor for the *Wisconsin State Journal*, a leading Republican newspaper.[10]

Thwaites stayed with the *State Journal* for ten years. During these years he sharpened his business and editorial skills while building a network of political contacts that proved to be essential in his later career. He also continued to pursue his historical interests, publishing sketches on Chief Oshkosh of the Menominee tribe, a history of Winnebago County, and various other pieces relating to local and state history. Much of Thwaites's research was conducted at the Historical Library in the south wing of the Wisconsin State Capitol, where he became acquainted with Lyman C. Draper, the chief administrator of the State Historical Society of Wisconsin. Through Draper's dedicated work the society was building one of the nation's finest collections of historical records. When Draper came to the society as secretary in 1854 the library contained 55 volumes. He built the collection to more than

110,000 books and, on his death in 1891, left to the society his large personal manuscript collection that he had acquired throughout his career. It was Draper's collecting, Frederick Jackson Turner wrote, that "had caused the Society to be recognized at home and abroad as the strongest in the West."[11]

Impressed by Thwaites's interest and enthusiasm, Draper chose Thwaites, who joined the society as assistant corresponding secretary in 1885, as his successor. When Draper retired he noted his pleasure "to feel assured that the laboring oar of the Society's success will fall into hands so competent by his culture, his tastes, his industry, and his habits as the gentleman you have approved."[12]

Thwaites manned the oars exceedingly well. For the next twenty-six years he guided the development of the society. Under his direction the society continued to grow and prosper and became the model for historical societies across the nation. Thwaites continued the aggressive acquisition policy of his predecessor. Moreover, the reading room was open and available to the public seven days a week beginning as early as 1889. A decade later a new Indiana limestone home for the collection was under construction at the foot of State Street. The new facility was built by the people of Wisconsin to house both the University of Wisconsin library and the burgeoning society collections and offices.

Thwaites used his statewide connections and political expertise to guide the appropriation process and the actual construction through to its completion in 1901. By 1902 the society had the finest building and was the second largest repository of books, manuscripts, and newspapers among state historical societies in the United States. This building continues to serve as the home of the State Historical Society of Wisconsin and its collections.[13]

Not only was Thwaites a skillful administrator, he was also a tireless promoter of the arts and humanities. In keeping with the reform spirit of his time, he considered a knowledge of the past to be essential to the workings of a democratic society. Thwaites was in demand as a speaker, and he encouraged the development of local historical societies, museums, and libraries at every opportunity. His zeal inspired one colleague to remark, "Energy, thy name is Thwaites."[14] Recognition for his public advocacy came in many ways, including the presidency of the American Library Association in 1900 and of the Mississippi Valley Historical Association (today's Organization of American Historians) in 1912.

Thwaites's most enduring legacy is his extensive body of scholarship. Drawing heavily upon the rich resources of the Draper Collection, his bibliography includes 120 edited volumes, 33 books, and 132 articles or

Reuben Gold Thwaites in his office at the State Historical Society of Wisconsin, 1892

State Historical Society of Wisconsin WHi (T53)99

short pamphlets. Most notable are the three major series that he edited: his definitive 73-volume *Jesuit Relations and Allied Documents*

(1896–1901), the 8-volume *Original Journals of Lewis and Clark* (1904–5), and the 32-volume compilation *Early Western Travels* (1904–6).

As Turner remarked in his memorial address, *Early Western Travels* provided scholars with access to many rare and significant accounts in a format that included an invaluable index. These volumes presented "a picture of the irresistible tide of American settlement flowing into the wilderness, of societies forming in the forests, of cities evolving almost under our gaze as we see them through the eyes of these travelers in successive years." *Jesuit Relations* and the *Original Journals of Lewis and Clark* made accessible to the public early travel accounts of the emerging American West. Taken together, the *Original Journals of Lewis and Clark, Jesuit Relations,* and *Early Western Travels* made Thwaites the "editorial authority" to whom students must turn if they were to study the frontier.[15]

In keeping with a standard feature of Thwaites's travel excursions, three members of the family accompanied him on the "Pilgrim" in the summer of 1894. Thwaites married Jessie Inwood Turvill on Christmas Day 1882. She was born in Madison on 22 November 1854. The Turvill family lived on a large farm on the southwest shore of Lake Monona and made their living selling flowers and vegetables to the residents of Madison. Acquired by the city of Madison in 1967, the former Turvill lakeside farm is today a popular meeting place to hike and picnic called Turville Park.[16]

Reuben and Jessie had two children: Fredrik T., who was born in 1884, and a daughter Margaret, who was born in 1888 and died at the age of two. Fred became a geologist and earned his Ph.D. at Wisconsin, where he spent most of his career as a member of the geology faculty and as the curator of the geological museum at the university. His summer adventure in the Ohio valley when he was ten years old included a visit to Kentucky's Big Bone Lick, one of the nation's best-known geological sites.

Jessie's brother, William Daniel Turvill, was born on 3 December 1850. He graduated from the University of Wisconsin with a degree in law in 1874 and studied medicine in the United States and Europe. Preferring to work with plants and flowers on the family farm, he returned to the Turvill property, where he spent the rest of his life. Turvill enjoyed the outdoors and was Thwaites's companion on a series of canoe trips on Wisconsin and Illinois rivers. The story of these adventures was told by Thwaites in *Historic Waterways: Six Hundred Miles of Canoeing Down the Rock, Fox, and Wisconsin Rivers*, published in 1888.[17]

Each of the "Pilgrim"'s passengers made a unique contribution to the trip. Jessie, referred to throughout by her author husband as "The W—" (wife), brought an extensive knowledge of the flowers and trees that characterized the landscape. Thwaites noted that her "enthusiasm for botany frequently takes us ashore."[18] The book's careful descriptions of the vegetation of the Ohio valley were undoubtedly contributed by Jessie and William.

William was an affable talker who frequently engaged in extended discussions with the colorful characters the four travelers encountered. Examples included a nitroglycerin hauler, a strawberry grower, and a shantyboater. Calling William "the Doctor" in his narrative, Thwaites used William's conversations to enrich his text.

Fred, known as "the Boy," brought youthful enthusiasm to the family's travels. "The Doctor" entertained Fred with stories and nature lessons. While Fred received little mention in the narrative, Thwaites gave his son the last word. The book ends with Fred looking pleadingly into his mother's face: "In tones half-choked with tears, he expressed the sentiment of all: 'Mother, is it really ended? Why can't we go back to Brownsville, and do it all over again?'"[19]

While young Fred's wish was not fulfilled, the Thwaites family did continue to take family vacations. Summer adventures took them through much of the United States from Virginia to California; they also visited Canada, Cuba, Panama, and made several trips to Europe. The center of professional and family life, however, was Madison, Wisconsin. They lived on Langdon Street, within walking distance of the State Historical Society of Wisconsin, until 1910 when the family moved to a newly built home on the Turvill estate. Madison was neither a village nor a city but "a neighborhood of friendly families both from the University and the state capitol—a place where town and gown mingled unenviously and where the good of the community was the concern of all."[20]

When Thwaites died suddenly of heart disease on 22 October 1913, the residents of the capital mourned the passing of "Wisconsin's most noted historian." Those attending his funeral included University of Wisconsin president Charles Van Hise, faculty and colleagues from the University of Wisconsin, which had awarded Thwaites an honorary L.L.D. degree in 1904, and numerous friends from the community. Two months later at a public ceremony held in the state capitol and conducted by Gov. Francis E. McGovern, Thwaites's old friend Frederick Jackson Turner delivered a lengthy memorial address in Thwaites's honor.[21]

Thwaites receives only passing notice in historical studies today. In his study of the historical profession in the United States, John Higham characterized Thwaites as "a former newspaperman with the mind of an entrepreneur."[22] This description ignores Thwaites's important role in building a new kind of institution—the state-supported historical society. Wisconsin led the way, and Thwaites came to embody the public-minded builder of cultural institutions. His leadership reflected the times as citizens formed organizations and discussion groups in the late nineteenth century, directing their attention to a host of civic issues ranging from child labor to consumer protection to public education. David P. Thelen described this movement in his book, *The New Citizenship: Origins of Progressivism in Wisconsin, 1885–1900*, a time when a spirit of cooperation across class lines helped to make Wisconsin a leading state in the Progressive movement.

While he is not included in Thelen's analysis, Thwaites was a tireless advocate of public libraries, museums, and local historical associations who exemplified these cooperative reform stirrings. Clifford L. Lord, who served the State Historical Society of Wisconsin as executive director from 1946 to 1958, considered Thwaites to be the "father of the progressive (or 'Western') historical society." His contribution, wrote Lord, is one that remains substantially unrecognized. Noting that Thwaites shunned publicity, Lord maintained that it was he "who wedded progressivism to the historical society" and, in so doing, was "the father of the institution we know today."[23]

Thwaites's most important scholarly contributions were his multi-volume editions of the *Jesuit Relations*, the *Original Journals of Lewis and Clark*, and *Early Western Travels*. Each set has been issued in a reprint edition in recent years. Louise Phelps Kellogg, who later became the first woman to serve as president of the Organization of American Historians, was a member of Thwaites's staff and worked closely with him on *Early Western Travels* and the Lewis and Clark journals. She considered Thwaites to be the best editor in the United States and said that:

> He taught me my trade—the trade of editing, not making, careful research in individual histories—all the niceties that go to make up a worthy volume of documents. . . . He had fine estimates of historical values, the importance of seemingly small things in their revelation of personality. He loved men and women; he liked a good story; was a prince of raconteurs.[24]

In his book, *The American Historian*, Harvey Wish noted the friendship between Thwaites and Turner, describing both as frontier historians. Wish wrote that Thwaites "put all students of the West in his debt" by his monumental series, *Early Western Travels*. In a monographic study of the Lewis and Clark journals, Paul Russell Cutright described Thwaites as an indefatigable scholar whose eight-volume work continues to serve "as the basic, indispensable source for all Lewis and Clark scholars." Stephen E. Ambrose described Thwaites's editorial work as "outstanding," noting that Thwaites's edition of the journals is "an American classic." Yet another acknowledgment of the lasting importance of the work done nearly one hundred years ago by Thwaites came in 1967 when Joseph P. Donnelly, S.J., published a book to bring the 73-volume *Jesuit Relations and Allied Documents* up-to-date.[25]

In 1991 the humanities councils of the six states along the Ohio River sponsored a traveling barge exhibit celebrating the history and life of the historic waterway. The barge's summerlong journey attracted huge crowds to a host of related activities designed to help the public understand and value the role of the Ohio River in our nation's past. It was my pleasure to edit a reader, *Always a River*, that accompanied the project. In my editorial work I returned to the original version of *Afloat on the Ohio*. Thwaites's references in the text to what he called "taking kodaks" piqued my curiosity. Since I have considerable interest in the use of photos to document history, I followed this lead. Christine Schelshorn of the Visual Materials Archive of the State Historical Society of Wisconsin led me to Thwaites's 1894 Ohio River album, and I began making plans to have the photographs published. In the meantime, Dan Hughes Fuller had begun to sort and catalog additions to the Thwaites Collection, which included the original negatives from the trip. The reproductions in this book and the prints in the related exhibition, *Afloat on the Ohio, 1894,* are the result of his careful technical work.

In his essay in *Always a River*, University of Illinois geographer John A. Jakle focused his interpretation on the changing landscape. He noted that the most evident change from the eighteenth to the nineteenth century was the high degree of industrialization and urbanization. This was particularly noticeable along the upper Ohio River where Thwaites observed that the "once beautiful banks" were marked by coal tipples, iron and steel mills, and enormous piles of "clay and iron offal." Thwaites's frequent references to locks and dams illustrated the substantial control that the engineering work of the United States Army Corps of Engineers brought to the Ohio. Railroad tracks paralleled the river, often on both sides, as the railroad bridges that spanned the Ohio in several places turned river towns into river-crossing towns. Villages whose names suggested the high ambitions of their founders were stagnant or in decay. Among those Thwaites mentioned were New Matamoras, Antiquity, Syracuse, Rosebud, Rome, Warsaw, and Troy.[26]

The photographs presented in this book are accompanied by passages from *Afloat on the Ohio*. This material supports the understanding that cameras capture places and people best. As Dan Fuller notes in his essay, "snapshots record moments," and for Thwaites the moments were those that seemed useful in recounting the story of his family's trip down the Ohio. Thus, while the book is rich with historical descriptions, the strength of the album is in the scenes that depict the substantial domestication of the Ohio.

Several of the photographs also present people in various activities, including boating and posing for the camera at sites along the river. The captions accompanying these images illustrate the paradoxical nature of Thwaites's nineteenth-century attitudes. As with his reports from earlier travels to the Southwest, Thwaites was prone to describe people who did not share his New England background and English heritage in harsh and prejudicial terms. Persons living in conditions of poverty were "poor whites" and "crackers," and African-American children were "picaninnies" and "sable elfs." At the Junction Iron Works near Steubenville, Ohio, the travelers were guests of an old friend, the superintendent of the mill, W. H. Bradley. Thwaites reported that the company limited the number of Hungarians and Slavs in the mill to 10 percent of the workforce because of their tendency "to 'run the town' when sufficiently numerous to make it possible." These immigrants worked for low wages that they saved in order to return to Europe and retire. "This sort of competition," wrote Thwaites, "is fast degrading legitimate American labor."[27]

Ambiguities surface in his relationships with Native Americans. On the one hand Thwaites described the Indians of Wisconsin as shiftless, childlike, and foul-smelling; on the other, he developed positive relationships with tribal spokesmen as he gathered narrative and pictorial representations from them for the society's collection. Even as he conveyed the clichés and stereotypes reflecting the nativist attitudes of his times, he was doing pioneer work in the field of ethnic studies. In 1888, in cooperation with the history department of the University of Wisconsin, he launched a project to study "the origin and status of foreign groups in Wisconsin." While the project was never completed, several papers were published and an initial survey was conducted. Almost fifty years before the pioneering immigration studies of Marcus Lee Hansen, Theodore C. Blegen, and Carl Wittke, Thwaites reported on the great variety of foreign groups in Wisconsin. In a conclusion remarkably advanced for his day he noted: "We are slowly building up in America a composite nationality that is neither English nor continental, but partakes of all—it is to be hoped, the best of all."[28]

Reuben Gold Thwaites was an editor, writer, administrator, and advocate for the study of American history. He was also an amateur photographer. His round images of the Ohio River in 1894 provide remarkable visual evidence of what life was like one hundred years ago.

NOTES

1. Reuben Gold Thwaites, *Afloat on the Ohio: An Historical Pilgrimage of a Thousand Miles in a Skiff, from Redstone to Cairo* (Chicago: Way and Williams, 1897). Redstone was the early name for Brownsville. It was the site of a British fort that was established in 1752. An extended essay, "A Day on Braddock's Road," on the family's visit to nearby Great Meadows, where George Washington and Virginia troops clashed with the French in 1754, and the adjacent site of Gen. Edward Braddock's death in 1755 is found in Reuben Gold Thwaites, *How George Rogers Clark Won the Northwest and Other Essays in Western History* (Chicago: A. C. McClurg and Co., 1903), 277–95.

2. Reuben Gold Thwaites, *On the Storied Ohio: An Historical Pilgrimage of a Thousand Miles in a Skiff, from Redstone to Cairo* (Chicago: A. C. McClurg and Co., 1903), xiv. This is the issue of *Afloat on the Ohio* published with a new title and preface; Thwaites, *Afloat on the Ohio,* xi, 317.

3. Turner and the frontier thesis have received major attention in recent years as the field of western history has taken on new life. An insightful study of attitudes about the closing of the frontier is David M. Wrobel, *The End of American Exceptionalism: Frontier Anxiety from the Old West to the New Deal* (Lawrence: University Press of Kansas, 1993). Walter Nugent provides a useful analysis of present-day understandings in his essay, "Where Is the American West? Report on a Survey," *Montana History* 42 (summer 1992): 2–23.

4. *Brownsville* (Pa.) *Clipper,* 17 May 1894. Thwaites noted this visit by a reporter in his diary.

5. Frederick Jackson Turner, *Reuben Gold Thwaites: A Memorial Address* (Madison: State Historical Society of Wisconsin, 1914), 38; Ray Allen Billington, *Frederick Jackson Turner: Historian, Scholar, Teacher* (New York: Oxford University Press, 1973), 35; *Wisconsin State Journal,* 30 Dec. 1884, 9 Jan. 1885.

6. Thwaites, *Afloat on the Ohio,* xiii, 301. Thwaites kept meticulous records. For example, he noted that each ticket from Milwaukee to Pittsburgh cost $15.92. The shipping charges for the "Pilgrim" were $3.97, and he tipped the freight agent $1.00. Thwaites Diary, vol. 1, Reuben G. Thwaites Papers, Archives Division, State Historical Society of Wisconsin (hereafter cited as Thwaites Papers).

It is likely that the "Pilgrim" was built by William and his brother Thomas. In the late 1860s they studied boat-building in New England and then set up a boatyard where they built more than two thousand boats. They sold them for use on the lakes in and around Madison. *Wisconsin State Journal,* 22 Jan. 1867.

7. Thwaites, *Afloat on the Ohio,* 204.

8. Brian Coe and Paul Gates, *The Snapshot Photograph: The Rise of Popular Photography, 1888–1939* (London: Ash and Grant, 1977), 18; Susan Sontag, *On Photography* (New York: Dell Books, 1977), 9–10.

9. Richard Chalfen, "Studies in the Home Mode of Visual Communication," *Working Papers in Communication and Culture* 1 (spring 1978): 39.

10. The most accurate obituary is found in the *Wisconsin State Journal,* 23 Oct. 1913; Turner, *Reuben Gold Thwaites,* 15–16. Turner does not mention the influence of growing up in a single-parent household. Details on the separation and divorce are found in a set of corre-

spondence between Jack Holzheuter and Steve Gilmour dated 15 and 24 Oct. 1980, General Correspondence, Thwaites Papers.

11. Turner, *Reuben Gold Thwaites,* 20.

12. Ibid., 19.

13. "Report of Committee on Methods of Organization and Work on the Part of State and Local Historical Societies," *Annual Report of the American Historical Association* 1 (1950), 249–325. See also Clifford Lee Lord and Carl Ubbelohde, *Clio's Servant: The State Historical Society of Wisconsin, 1846–1954* (Madison: State Historical Society of Wisconsin, 1967).

14. L. S. Hanks to Reuben Thwaites, 21 Feb. 1913, Archives Division, 27/1/3, Box 17, State Historical Society of Wisconsin.

15. Turner, *Reuben Gold Thwaites,* 48, 49. In his review of *Jesuit Relations,* Theodore Roosevelt called Thwaites "one of a new band of Western historians who, during the last decade, have opened up an entirely new field of historical study." *Catholic World* 44 (1896): 812.

16. The area was called the Monona Assembly Grounds in the late nineteenth century. *Wisconsin State Journal,* 26 Dec. 1924 (Thomas Turvill obituary). Jessie Turvill Thwaites died on 14 Aug. 1938. One of her major accomplishments was her leadership in support of relief work during World War I. Ibid., 22 Jan. 1967.

17. Reuben Gold Thwaites, *Historic Waterways: Six Hundred Miles of Canoeing Down the Rock, Fox, and Wisconsin Rivers* (Chicago: A. C. McClurg, 1888); *Wisconsin State Journal,* 16, 24 Oct. 1916. Another travel narrative, *Our Cycling Tour in England: From Canterbury to Dartmoor Forest, and Back by Way of Bath, Oxford, and the Thames Valley,* was published in 1892. A similar album of round Kodaks is found in the Thwaites Collection.

18. Thwaites, *Afloat on the Ohio,* 42.

19. Ibid., 295.

20. Dan Fuller, "Thwaites Collection: Nitrate Negatives 1891–1907" (1992), Visual Materials Archive, State Historical Society of Wisconsin; Reuben G. Thwaites to F. J. Turner, 10 Oct. 1910, Frederick J. Turner Papers, Henry E. Huntington Library and Art Gallery, Los Angeles; Louise Phelps Kellogg, "The Passing of a Great Teacher—Frederick Jackson Turner," *The Historical Outlook* 23 (Oct. 1932): 272.

21. *Madison Democrat,* 23 Oct. 1913; *Wisconsin State Journal,* 20 Dec. 1913.

22. John Higham, *History: Professional Scholarship in America* (Baltimore: Johns Hopkins University Press, 1983), 18.

23. Clifford L. Lord, "Reuben Gold Thwaites and the Progressive

Historical Society," The (Clarence M.) Burton Lecture, Historical Society of Michigan, 1963, p. 15.

24. Louise Phelps Kellogg to C. M. Ewing, 22 June 1938, Louise Phelps Kellogg Papers, Archives Division, State Historical Society of Wisconsin.

25. Harvey Wish, *The American Historian: A Social-Intellectual History of the Writing of the American Past* (New York: Oxford University Press, 1960), 184; Paul Russell Cutright, *A History of the Lewis and Clark Journals* (Norman: University of Oklahoma Press, 1976), viii; Stephen E. Ambrose, *Undaunted Courage: Meriwether Lewis, Thomas Jefferson, and the Opening of the American West* (New York: Simon and Schuster, 1996), 470; Joseph P. Donnelly, S.J., *Thwaites' Jesuit Relations: Errata and Addenda* (Chicago: Loyola University Press, 1967).

26. John A. Jakle, "The Ohio River Revisited," in Robert L. Reid, ed., *Always a River: The Ohio River and the American Experience* (Bloomington: Indiana University Press, 1991), 32–66. See also the essay by Darrel E. Bigham on the economic history of the Ohio valley and Leland R. Johnson on the work of the United States Army Corps of Engineers. The latter's *The Ohio River Division: U.S. Army Corps of Engineers: The Central Command* (Louisville, Ky.: United States Army

Corps of Engineers, Louisville District, 1992) is an expanded treatment of this subject.

27. Thwaites, *Afloat on the Ohio,* 44, 45. The Junction Iron Works was a subsidiary of the Laughlin and Junction Steel Company. When US Steel was formed in 1901 it became the Mingo Plant of the Carnegie Illinois Division. The plant continues in operation today as a division of the Wheeling-Pittsburgh Steel Corporation.

28. *Madison Democrat,* 4 Nov. 1887; Rudolph J. Vecoli, "European Americans: From Immigrants to Ethnics," in William H. Cartwright and Richard L. Watson, Jr., eds., *The Reinterpretation of American History and Culture* (Washington, D.C.: National Council for the Social Studies, 1973), 82–83; "Preliminary Notes on the Distribution of Foreign Groups in Wisconsin," *Annual Report of the Secretary of the State Historical Society of Wisconsin* (1990), 57–63.

O n 4 May 1894 Reuben Gold Thwaites began an expedition in a fifteen-foot rowboat with his wife, son, and brother-in-law on the Monongahela River in western Pennsylvania. The hardy group spent thirty-eight days traveling a thousand miles down the Monongahela and Ohio Rivers to the Mississippi River. Along the way Thwaites took eighty-four snapshots with his #2 Kodak camera, and, once home, had the film developed and put the prints in an album. Although such a trip was as extraordinary in 1894 as it would be today, the taking of snapshots seems perfectly normal. This use of photography, however, was a novelty then because snapshot photography was less than six years old.[1]

Luckily, Thwaites was a careful historian who not only documented and preserved his photograph albums, but also most of his negatives as well, making possible the high quality of the illustrations in this book. This photographic material, along with Thwaites's journals, financial records, and published books, makes it possible to gauge his motivations for photographing.[2] A comparison with previous photographic techniques shows how the technology of the #2 Kodak was suited to Thwaites's purposes.

Except for the lack of full color, the photographs taken along the Ohio River in 1894 have more in common technically with contemporary snapshots than they do with their immediate predecessors. Aesthetically, they often differ so much from both as to be unique. What follows are explanations of their standing in the history of photographic technique, Thwaites's use of them, and some analysis of why they look the way they do.

OUTDOOR PHOTOGRAPHY BEFORE 1888

The first extant photograph is a farmyard scene taken by Joseph Nicéphore Niépce through an upper window at his estate in France. The materials Niépce used were so insensitive to light that this vague and faded image required an exposure time of eight hours when it was made around 1827.[3]

Over the decades the sensitivity of photographic materials increased, so that by 1878 the most popular technique of the day, wet collodion on glass, usually required an exposure of just seconds. However, to make exposures in the field as Thwaites would do sixteen years later on the Ohio, the wet-plate photographer had to bring along a portable darkroom supplied with chemicals—most were poisonous or flammable—and a quantity of water. The difficulty was that the glass plate had to be sensitized just before exposure in the camera, itself a large contraption mounted on a tripod. While damp, the plate was sensitive, but, once dry, it was nearly dead to light. So making a series of exposures outdoors involved as much as sixty pounds of equipment and hours of exertion. The first hour would be spent setting up the darkroom and sensitizing and exposing a plate, which straightaway had to go through a developing and washing process. Allowing fifty minutes for the preparation, exposure, and processing of subsequent plates meant that about nine exposures could be made in eight hours by an unassisted photographer. An assistant, a pack animal, and some running water nearby could speed up the operation, but, pared to essentials, nine exposures in eight hours was quick work for the outdoor photographer in 1878.[4]

By 1880 the cumbersome collodion wet-plate process was becoming obsolete. By then factories in Europe and America were producing gelatin dry plates that were ten times as sensitive and could be exposed months after manufacture and developed months after exposure, eliminating the necessity of portable darkrooms. The average photographer's burden outdoors was reduced to a large-format camera, tripod, plates, and accessories. A moderately sized outfit weighed thirty pounds, not counting the plates brought along for the day's shooting. It was physically possible to expose up to four plates a minute. At that rate, an unassisted, hyperactive dry-plate photographer could make 1,920 exposures in eight hours. Glass is heavy, though, and the number of plates and light-tight holders needed for such a marathon would weigh six hundred pounds.

THE KODAK SYSTEM

In 1888 George Eastman, a manufacturer of gelatin dry plates, introduced a simple camera that, from the average user's perspective, did away with glass plates and darkrooms altogether. The fully loaded Kodak with its one hundred-exposure roll of stripping film weighed only one pound and ten ounces.[5] With it even a child could make up to eight exposures a minute. When all the photos were taken, the camera could be returned to the factory where the film was developed, printed, and a new roll installed. To apply the eight-hour test to this apparatus, consider that a Kodak user operating at fever pitch would shoot one hundred exposures in thirteen and a half minutes. Given five minutes to reload after each roll—a darkroom would still be necessary for this—eight hours of constant camera work would yield 2,600 exposures. Although this produces just 35 percent more than the dry-plate photographer, it saves more than 99 percent of the weight. Twenty-six rolls of film weighed just three and a quarter pounds.[6]

This shortening of time and lightening of the load made photographic expeditions like Thwaites's possible. All at once amateurs could make a simple pastime out of what had been a skilled and sometimes onerous profession. In its essentials—except, again, for the lack of color—the system of photography introduced by Eastman is the same used by millions today: exposure after exposure recorded by a small, lightweight camera on a roll of film—without reloading for each exposure, without tripods, dark cloths, and portable darkrooms—which is sent away for developing and printing. More than a century later the world still lives in the era of Eastman's slogan, "You push the button, we do the rest."

A NEW BREED OF PHOTOGRAPHER

The introduction of the Kodak led to the emergence of a new and rapidly growing breed of photographer who made pictures, not as a professional for hire, but for personal use as documents of family, business, and travel. The resulting pictures answered needs that commercially available work could not. The *1894 Kodak Catalogue* identified the main drawback of commercial photography:

The trouble is in the "point of view." The pictures may be technically excellent, but the photographer failed to catch the particular thing in which you were interested or the view that pleased you the most. The Kodaker takes pictures *from his own point of view.*[7]

Amateur photographers would not usurp the role of professional photographers in the studio or at weddings, funerals, and other grand events. Instead, amateurs would document places, activities, and subjects that the professional photographers never would consider:

Are you a bicyclist, canoeist or yachtsman? Are you an artist, engineer, architect or machinist? Do you teach, preach or edit? Are you a lawyer, doctor, manufacturer or merchant? Then you should be able to take pictures from your "own point of view."

Would it be to your advantage in business if you could take a picture at an outlay of a few minutes' time and a few cents in money? Would it be better for your health if you indulged occasionally in a pleasant recreation that would take your mind from the cares of the office? Are you fond of good pictures? Then buy a Kodak.[8]

This sales pitch convinced hundreds of thousands of people in the upper and middle classes, among whom was the head of the State Historical Society of Wisconsin, Reuben Gold Thwaites, to purchase a Kodak.

Reuben Gold Thwaites and Photography

Like most Americans at the end of the nineteenth century, Thwaites was no stranger to photography. Every few years he would hire a photographer to make portraits of his family or photographs of his house. When he traveled he bought commercially produced photographs or postcards of the places he visited and pasted them into albums upon his return. It was also his habit to keep a journal of all he saw and thought while away. His historical training and broad interests were reflected in his journal entries that were often rewritten into articles for midwestern newspapers such as the *Chicago Tribune, Milwaukee Sentinel,* and *Minneapolis Tribune.* His most extensive expeditions resulted in books that took the form of travelogues.

In April 1889 Thwaites bought a dry-plate camera for thirty dollars, although it seems that its first use was to make copies of historic portrait paintings for reproduction in a book. Initially he may have engaged someone to operate the camera for him. However, account book entries for the remainder of 1889 and throughout 1890 suggest that by this time he was making his own pictures and perhaps developing the negatives himself.

In August 1890 Thwaites took a canoe trip on the Brule River in northern Wisconsin with his brother-in-law, William Daniel Turvill, and his nephew, Kent Turvill Woods. Woods took pictures with a 4 x 5-inch glass-plate camera. They met other people on the river who had cameras with them as well. In a letter to his wife, Jessie Turvill Thwaites, dated 12 August 1890, Reuben wrote:

> One of the ladies had a Kodak, and took several shots at us & as ill luck would have it, we had on this stretch the only accident on the trip. William and I, who were together, missed our hold on the bottom, and our bow being swept suddenly into the stream we went flying back again, broadside, and before we could recover ourselves, our craft had swamped to the gunwales. One of the Kodak pictures took us in the very midst of this disaster. However, we finally reached the top. I bowed to the ladies, who returned to us one of our bundles which we had lost overboard further downstream, and they went ahead, out of view, leaving us to creep along in our own fashion.[9]

Clearly this encounter with the Kodak camera impressed Thwaites (and embarrassed him as well). He had had enough experience with dry-plate cameras to know how difficult it would be to capture such a scene with any camera but a Kodak.

THE #2 KODAK CAMERA

The original Kodak camera of 1888 was succeeded by the slightly improved #1 Kodak of 1889.[10] At the time photographic prints were generally made by contact printing, which meant that the negatives' sizes were also the sizes of the final prints. Compared to the 4 x 5, 5 x 7, or 8 x 10-inch negatives produced by large-format view cameras in common use, the 2½-inch negatives produced by the first Kodak cameras made tiny prints. Another drawback, along with the small prints, was inherent in one of the best features of these cameras: their ability to make a hundred exposures without reloading. People found this number excessive and confusing. To shoot such a long roll of film could take months, and, over such a length of time, one might begin to wonder whether the camera was indeed working as it should. Moreover, the cameras lacked a mechanism to count exposures, making it impossible to know how many pictures remained to be shot without keeping notes. The cameras also lacked viewfinders. Instead, a V-shape was embossed into the top of the camera, indicating, in a general way, how much of the scene was to appear in the picture. To amend some of these faults the #2 Kodak was introduced in October 1889.

The #2 Kodak was the last of the first generation of Kodak roll film cameras, and it made a larger negative (3½ inches) on a shorter roll

#2 Kodak camera

Courtesy George Eastman House

of film (sixty exposures). Its deluxe features were a small reflecting viewfinder and three stops to compensate for varying light levels, but in most ways it was simply a larger version of the previous Kodaks. Like them, its focus could not be adjusted, and so it depended on a wide lens, taking in nearly 70° of view, to provide adequate focus from three and a half feet to infinity.[11]

17 APRIL 1891, KODAK $35.00

The day before boarding the Cunard steamship *Etruria* for England, Reuben Gold Thwaites bought a #2 Kodak camera in New York City. The purchase is prominent because all evidence suggests that Reuben and Jessie Thwaites were extremely careful with their money, and figures as high as $35.00 are rare in the family's account book. Entries were made each time a penny was spent to buy marbles for their son Fredrik or twenty-five cents for a toothbrush or haircut for Reuben. The entry for 28 March 1888, recording seventy-five cents spent for a book of poetry, is annotated, "in a moment of weakness," in Jessie's hand. Larger expenses such as the maid's two-week wage of $5.00 or $8.50 for a ton of stove coal were carefully balanced against Reuben's $2,000.00 yearly salary and the additional $500.00 earned mainly from mortgages, interest, and his writing. Monthly averages were calculated, and each year's surplus noted with satisfaction.

When it came to travel, although they still counted every penny, the Thwaiteses were capable of spending large amounts. For their trip to Britain in 1891, much of which was spent touring by bicycle, the Thwaiteses spent $135.00 for Jessie's bicycle, $90.00 for Reuben's, $235.00 for two round-trip steamship fares across the Atlantic, $32.93 for professionally produced photographs, $35.00 for the #2 Kodak, and $6.29 for developing and printing the pictures.

For Thwaites these were business expenses that would produce a product, a book. *Our Cycling Tour in England* (1892) strictly followed the content and sequence of Thwaites's journal and his album of one hundred Kodak photographs.[12] However, commercial photographs were used in the book instead of those Thwaites took. Although he did have lantern slides made from selected negatives, which he presented during a lecture on his travels in England, he used the snapshots mainly for reference and as a visual extension of his note taking. They were memory aids and sources for details he would call upon when writing the book's manuscript. The primary justification for photography with the Kodak was its efficiency as a tool for Thwaites the travel writer, despite its expense.

AFLOAT ON THE OHIO

In 1894 this pattern was repeated on the Ohio River trip. Day by day Thwaites took pictures with the #2 Kodak camera of river craft, people, and scenic views that particularly caught his attention. Each evening in camp he wrote in his journal what he had seen and heard that day. Once home in Wisconsin, he pasted the photographs into an album in chronological order and began working on a book manuscript, referring to the journal to confirm dates, locations, and captions. The result of his labors was *Afloat on the Ohio* (1897), which combined a travelogue with historical commentary appropriate to the places visited. As in the previous book, although many of the episodes could have been illustrated by reproductions of Thwaites's snapshots, they were not.[13]

Afloat on the Ohio was successful enough to be reprinted in 1903, with a new preface and the addition of photographic illustrations, as *On the Storied Ohio*.[14] Despite the close correspondence between Thwaites's Kodak photographs, his journal, and the book, all seven illustrations are reproductions of standard commercial photographs. Who chose the commercial photographs and why are questions difficult to answer a century later, although a comparison of the commercial view and the Kodak snapshot may provide some hints.

State Historical Society of Wisconsin WHi(X3)50716

"Public Landing, Cincinnati, Ohio"

NEAR THE LEVEL OF THE FLOOD

In the preface to *Afloat on the Ohio* Thwaites wrote, "In making our historical pilgrimage we might more easily have 'steamboated' the river,—to use a verb in local vogue; but, from the deck of a steamer, scenes take on a different aspect than when viewed from near the level of the flood."[15] This is an explanation of why an educated, well-to-do man took his family on a long, wet, cold, and muddy camping trip down a river in a small boat, and it also explains the difference between the photographs he took on that trip and those that he bought.

A good example of the latter is the postcard "Public Landing, Cincinnati, Ohio," which Thwaites pasted in the back of the album containing his own photographs. This standard commercial view,

although not a particularly attractive photograph, follows conventions established long before the invention of photography. It obeys the compositional rule of thirds, which divides the scene with lines into three horizontal and three vertical sections. In this scheme the horizon should begin two thirds of the way from the bottom or two thirds of the way from the top, but never at the midpoint. In addition, the principal object of interest, in this case the massive bridge piling just right of center, should be placed near the intersection of two of the division lines, again never in the middle. Another convention dictates that the point of view should be level with the principal object of interest, that is, level with the bridge's roadbed. This high, balanced, and static view

23

"Vanishing View of Cincinnati"

The horizon is almost exactly in the middle, and the bridge, still the principal object of interest, hangs darkly and precariously over the scene. In traditional terms the photograph is unbalanced. The foreground of dull, gray water, supplying more mood than information, occupies half the frame, much more than its share according to the rule of thirds. All the points of interest, the bridge and the steamboats moored beyond it, crowd on the left, weighing it down and leaving the right end of the bridge's span hanging in ambiguous space.

The characteristics of these two photographs define the major differences between large-format photography with the view camera and roll film photography with the snapshot camera, differences that hold true today. Large-format cameras, although bulky and technically demanding to operate, can provide extensive detail. Further examination of "Public Landing, Cincinnati, Ohio" yields more and more information about the waterfront: steamboats, wharf boats, houseboats, a fishing skiff, freight and driftwood on the muddy shore, the bridge, and the warehouses facing the landing. A close examination of "Vanishing View of Cincinnati" will dredge up some detail from the murk—the sterns of the moored steamboats, a second bridge nearly lost in the distance—but, on the whole, long observation serves only to confirm first impressions. Large-format photographs record scenes

of the subject is consistent with the constraints the large-format view camera, tripod, dark cloth, and handful of plates put on the dry-plate photographer.

Thwaites's "Vanishing View of Cincinnati" [see above and page 71], while taken of a very similar subject, could hardly be more different.

composed of many details. Snapshots record moments. It is as if the time spent by the large-format photographer selecting a vantage point, setting up the camera, and composing the scene on the ground glass requires a similarly measured look from the viewer. Thwaites's snapshot, made in an instant as his boat rushed downstream from the city, conveys its message more quickly, giving the viewer an immediate impression of what it was like to have passed under a huge bridge in a small boat on a stormy day.

THE GREAT CIRCLE

Of course the one great distinction of Thwaites's snapshots is that they are circular. This sets them apart, not only from rectangular photographs but also from the great majority of all visual representations. Although the circular format made appearances through the centuries, it was usually in conjunction with necessarily circular forms in architecture or objects such as coins, seals, shields, plates, or the backs of hand mirrors. In general, rectangles of various proportions, and, to a lesser extent, squares, have always been the dominant shapes of pictures.[16]

Camera lenses naturally produce circular images, and several of the earliest daguerreotype cameras took circular plates.[17] These cameras often looked like telescopes and, like telescopes, wasted little of the image-forming abilities of their lenses. As lenses improved in quality and decreased in price, image quality took precedence over raw image area, and rectangular masks were used in cameras to hide the distortions found at the edges of the circle and to produce negatives with the more popular shape.

Why did the first three mass-produced Kodak cameras make circular negatives? The *1894 Kodak Catalogue* identifies one advantage of the circular format this way: "as the image is round it requires no care to hold the camera square with the object."[18] Since the early Kodak cameras were difficult to aim accurately, it was an advantage to let the technicians in Rochester square the horizon of the picture with the edges of the photographic paper while printing, although this added another step to an already complicated system of processing. Another rationale was that since the lens was one of the most expensive parts to manufacture, it should be used to its fullest. The #2 Kodak's $3\frac{1}{4}$-inch lens made slightly more than a $3\frac{1}{2}$-inch circle, but a more expensive $4\frac{1}{2}$-inch lens would have had to be used to cover adequately a $3\frac{1}{2}$-inch square. However, film was expensive, too, and a series of circular exposures wasted much more film than a similar series of square exposures.

These technical explanations for Eastman's choice, while true, may not tell the whole story. The circular format also had novelty value. As has been repeated often, Eastman chose the invented word "Kodak" as his trademark because it was short, easy to pronounce, and did not "resemble anything in the art and cannot be associated with anything in the art except the Kodak."[19] At first the circular format functioned in the same way. Kodak pictures were instantly recognizable and were unlikely to be confused with the product of most other cameras. Of course the grand success of the cameras invited imitators, and in 1893 the Blair Camera Company of Boston introduced the Petite Kamarette, and Alfred C. Kemper of Chicago introduced the Kombi. Both made circular negatives.[20] Although the trademark "Kodak" was owned by Eastman, the circle was not.

By 1897 all three circular Kodak cameras had been discontinued and replaced by cameras producing a variety of square and rectangular negatives. Thwaites, too, switched to a square format, buying a #2 Bullet in 1897, which he took with him on a five-month European tour.

REUBEN GOLD THWAITES AS PHOTOGRAPHER

Most of the photographs Thwaites took with his #2 Kodak are interesting. Some are even beautiful, which seems surprising given the limitations of a camera that could not be aimed with precision or focused at all. Although the camera was simple to operate, mistakes were easy to make, and on the Ohio River trip Thwaites made just two. Early on he created a double exposure, and later the shutter was pressed accidently, recording the side of the boat and a slice of sky at a crazy angle. Overall, Thwaites seems to have followed the instruction book carefully, photographing with the sun behind him on bright days and avoiding quickly moving subjects and dark shade. His photography certainly benefited from the habits of regularity and care he had followed in his journals and account books. Being careful, however, does not guarantee interesting pictures.

Thwaites also had a good eye, or, at least, had had a clear idea of what subjects should make good pictures in a conventional sense. His photographs of William and Fred at Big Bone Lick, Kentucky [page 76], and the fishermen at Cypress Creek, Indiana [page 91], are examples of Thwaites's good judgment working in concert with the light available and the qualities of the camera to produce exceptionally beautiful images. The photos probably would have been just as lovely had they been composed in a square or rectangular format.

Many other photographs taken on the Ohio River succeed because of the concentrating power of the circular composition. Somehow placing the object of interest dead center (in absolute disobedience to the rule of thirds) can make it especially poignant or mysterious.

Examples include the three boys in the crude boat [page 40], the man with nitroglycerin [page 45], Reuben aboard the "Pilgrim" [page 48], the Indian Mound in Moundsville, West Virginia [page 54], and Jessie and Fred at the mouth of the Saline River in Illinois [page 100]. Although unsophisticated, this bull's-eye composition is an honest acceptance of the power of the circle's center.

Finally, some of Thwaites's Ohio River photographs satisfy the tastes of a later era. The foreboding darkness and imbalance of the vanishing view of Cincinnati [page 71], previously mentioned, seems to date it as a pictorialist composition, perhaps by Alvin Langdon Coburn, from 1912 or later, at least eighteen years after its time. The Magrittesque humor of three men in the boat on the outskirts of Wheeling, West Virginia [page 51], makes it seem like a frame from a silent film of Buster Keaton or one of André Kertész's street photographs from the late 1920s.

The most interesting and disturbing of the pictures cannot be pigeonholed because the vision they present is unique. For example, the crowd of men and boys have probably come out of curiosity to watch as Reuben, Jessie, Fred, and William shove off into the Indian Kentucky River on 27 May 1894 [page 80]. Looking at the image today, what is most evident is the #2 Kodak's strange vision that manages to stretch and blur the man on the left and the boy on the right in the foreground and turn the trees in the background into a smudge, while rendering faces in the middle ground sharp and the mud the men stand on as rich as chocolate. They stare with hands on hips, a posture of curiosity or perhaps disapproval. Similarly, the oil wells at Witten's Bottom, Ohio [page 57], are transformed into a bizarre landscape by the camera. Perhaps Thwaites intended to base the picture's composition on the three oil derricks that march in line from near left to distant right. The background, however, has swallowed all but the first derrick, leaving a composition weighted almost entirely on the left third with its looming derrick, ramshackle house, and a man digging. To top it off, strange wires zoom up from the ground and into the sky and disappear out of the frame, creating an unusual and memorable photograph.

THE END OF THE FAD

Like most fads, the popularity of the early circular Kodaks died down, but the market George Eastman had discovered and energetically developed for consumer photography increased. As we have seen, Thwaites kept up with the young industry, buying a #2 Bullet in 1897 and his last camera, a #3 Folding Pocket Kodak, in 1901. This succession of cameras took him increasingly further from the pictures he made in the summer of 1894 along the Ohio River.

Better viewfinders and lenses with longer focal lengths meant that Thwaites could stand farther from his subjects and compose his photographs more carefully. The 3¼ x 4¼-inch rectangle of his #3 Folding Pocket Kodak encouraged compositions more like that of the postcard view "Public Landing, Cincinnati, Ohio" than his circular snapshots of the Ohio. The larger negatives and sharper lens also meant that more detail would be recorded, but perhaps less atmosphere.

Thwaites's natural inclination in life and in photography was toward care and precision, characteristics that yielded postcardlike perfection from the #3 Folding Pocket Kodak. The #2 Kodak, however, could not produce anything like a postcard, no matter how carefully handled. The circular format broke the mold of traditional composition, and using it on the fly while floating downstream made careful aiming impossible. (One wonders whether Thwaites intended to include the oar appearing in the foreground of several pictures.) The happy result was that Thwaites's carefulness prevented him from making many serious technical mistakes, and the idiosyncrasies of the camera make his photographs worthy of our attention a hundred years later.

NOTES

1. In this essay, snapshot is taken to mean not just an instantaneous photograph, but an instantaneous photograph that can be taken quickly by an amateur photographer as part of a series, without reloading the camera and with a minimum of manipulation. The move from the dry-plate camera—even a relatively convenient handheld camera carrying multiple plates within its body—to the Kodak roll film camera introduced in July 1888 was the technological leap that made the snapshot possible.

2. Reuben Gold Thwaites Collection, Mss. VJ, State Historical Society of Wisconsin. Written records of the Thwaites family (including letters, diaries, account books, and manuscripts) are housed in the Manuscript Archives of the society. Photographic material is housed in the society's Visual Materials Archive.

3. Niépce used a pewter plate coated with a light-sensitive bitumen. The photograph is now in the Gernsheim Collection of the Humanities Research Center, University of Texas, Austin. It is widely reproduced in histories of photography, such as Beaumont Newhall, *The History of Photography: From 1839 to the Present* (New York: Museum of Modern Art, 1982) and Naomi Rosenblum, *A World History of Photography* (New York: Abbeville Press, 1984).

4. These are approximate times for a process that varied with each wet-plate photographer. Some were able to keep plates wet an hour or more before exposure and to postpone fixing and washing the devel-

oped plates for additional hours or even days. The surest method, however, was to process the plates as soon as possible. Various techniques are discussed in Edward Livingstone Wilson, *Wilson's Photographics: A Series of Lessons Accompanied by Notes, on All the Processes which Are Needful in the Art of Photography* (New York: Edward L. Wilson, 1881), 244–49.

5. At first Kodak cameras were supplied with stripping film, a gelatin emulsion upon a paper base. After development, an intricate operation was performed stripping the negative emulsion from the paper, attaching it to another layer of gelatin, and varnishing both sides with collodion. During the summer of 1889, Eastman's transparent film became commercially available, making the stripping film obsolete. The new film was a gelatin emulsion upon a clear base of cellulose nitrate. Although the composition of the clear plastic base has changed, this is the basic form of subsequent photographic films.

6. Although no still photographer in 1888 would use film as extravagantly as this eight-hour comparison suggests, experimenters in America and Europe were quick to recognize the ability of Eastman's film to make sequential photographs as the essential element in developing motion pictures. Douglas Collins, *The Story of Kodak* (New York: N. H. Abrams, 1990), Chapter 2, provides a good overview of the film's role in the birth of motion pictures.

7. *1894 Kodak Catalogue: Kodaks and Kodets* (Rochester, N.Y.: Eastman Kodak Co., 1894), 3.

8. Ibid., 3–4.

9. R. G. Thwaites to J. T. Thwaites, 12 Aug. 1890, Reuben Gold Thwaites Papers, Archives Division, State Historical Society of Wisconsin. The letter describes the Brule River and St. Croix Lake trip.

10. A good description of the early years at Kodak can be found in Brian Coe, *The Birth of Photography: The Story of the Formative Years, 1800–1900* (London: Ash and Grant, 1976) and Collins, *Story of Kodak.* Coe's *Cameras: From Daguerreotypes to Instant Pictures* (Gothenburg: Nordbok, 1978) contains good descriptions of the cameras themselves accompanied by fine illustrations.

11. The *1894 Kodak Catalogue,* 15, states that the #2 Kodak's $3\frac{1}{4}$ -inch lens had a working angle of 50°, but this is the angle of view such a lens would produce for a square fitted within the #2 Kodak's image circle. A more accurate figure would be the almost 70° angle of view for a square having the same area as the #2 Kodak's circular negative. For comparison, this corresponds to a 32mm lens for 35mm cameras.

12. Reuben Gold Thwaites, *Our Cycling Tour in England: From Canterbury to Dartmoor Forest, and Back by Way of Bath, Oxford, and the Thames Valley* (Chicago: A. C. McClurg, 1892).

13. Reuben Gold Thwaites, *Afloat on the Ohio: An Historical Pilgrimage of a Thousand Miles in a Skiff, from Redstone to Cairo* (Chicago: Way and Williams, 1897). The correspondence between the photographs and written records is not quite complete. The photograph of Jessie Thwaites holding the oars was omitted from the album and has been given an approximate date based on internal evidence. Three landscape photographs shot before 30 May are miscaptioned by Thwaites as having been shot farther downriver in June. There was also a gap in the photographic record from 15–24 May 1894, apparently due to stormy weather and time spent in a Cincinnati hotel. (On this trip, Thwaites used the camera to record scenes only along the river and nearby historic sites, not city scenes.)

14. *Afloat on the Ohio* was reprinted unchanged in 1900 by Doubleday and McClure of New York. Then it appeared as *On the Storied Ohio: An Historical Pilgrimage of a Thousand Miles in a Skiff, from Redstone to Cairo* (Chicago: A. C. McClurg, 1903).

15. Thwaites, *Afloat on the Ohio*, xii–xiii.

16. Rudolf Arnheim's *The Power of the Center: A Study of Composition in the Visual Arts* (Berkeley: University of California Press, 1982) is a fine discussion of pictorial composition with a particular emphasis on circular forms.

17. Carl August von Steinheil's camera of 1839 and Peter Wilhelm Friedrich Voigtlander's and Alexis Gaudin's cameras of 1841 are mentioned as producers of circular daguerreotypes in Coe, *Cameras*, 18.

18. *1894 Kodak Catalogue*, 15.

19. Eastman's English patent application as quoted in Collins, *Story of Kodak*, 55.

20. Coe, *Cameras*, 88, 125. The story of one camera's influence upon the design of another may be more complicated than indicated. R. D. Gray introduced a vest camera in 1885 that was produced by the thousands in several countries. Its most common form made six circular exposures on a circular (or octagonal) glass plate, and Eastman may have had knowledge of the camera before he introduced the Kodak in 1888.

The photographs that follow are reproductions of modern prints made by Dan Fuller from
original negatives exposed by Reuben Gold Thwaites in his #2 Kodak camera in 1894.
The short captions are adapted from those Thwaites wrote in his photograph album.
The longer texts, unless labeled otherwise, are excerpts from his book *Afloat on the Ohio.*

There were four of us pilgrims—my Wife, our Boy of ten and a half years, the Doctor, and I. My object in going—the others went for the outing—was to gather "local color" for work in Western history.

In making our historical pilgrimage we might more easily have "steamboated" the river, — to use a verb in local vogue; but, from the deck of a steamer, scenes take on a different aspect than when viewed from near the level of the flood; for a passenger by such a craft, the vistas of a winding stream change so rapidly that he does not realize how it seemed to the canoeist or flat-boatman of old; and there are too many modern distractions about such a mode of progress. To our minds, the manner of our going should as nearly as possible be that of the pioneer himself— hence our skiff, and our nightly camp in primitive fashion.

pp. xi, xii–xiii

(X3)49420

This is the only photograph not included in the album. The date and place were identified by negative number and internal evidence.

May 4 or 5

Jessie rowing

Monongahela River

May 5

Coal tipple

Monongahela River

near California, Pennsylvania

The Monongahela is a characteristic mountain trough. From an altitude of four or five hundred feet, the country falls in sharp steeps to a narrow alluvial bench, and then to a broad beach of shale and pebble; the slopes are broken, here and there, where deep, shadowy ravines come winding down, bearing muddy contributions to the greater flood.

Tipples of bituminous coal-shafts are ever in sight— begrimed scaffolds of wood and iron, arranged for dumping the product of the mines into both barges and railway cars. Either bank is lined with railways, in sight of which we shall almost continually float, all the way down to Cairo, nearly eleven hundred miles away. At each tipple is a miners' hamlet; a row of cottages or huts, cast in a common mold, either unpainted, or bedaubed with that cheap, ugly red with which one is familiar in railway bridges and rural barns.

pp. 6, 7

(X3)49421

oaling hamlets more or less deserted were frequent this morning—unpainted, window-less, ragged wrecks. At the inhabited mining villages, either close to the strand or well up on the hillside ledges, idle men were everywhere about. Women and boys and girls were stockingless and shoeless, and often dirty to a degree. But, when conversed with, we found them indepen-dent, respectful, and self-respecting folk. . . . There are old-fashioned Dutch ovens in nearly every yard, a few chickens, and often a shed for a cow, that is off on her daily climb over the neighboring hills.

pp. 10–11

May 5

Outdoor bake oven

Monongahela River

May 5

Coal Tipple on the Monongahela
near Clairton, Pennsylvania

reariest of all is a deserted mining village, and there are many such—the shaft having been worked out, or an unquenchable subterranean fire left to smolder in neglect. Here the tipple has fallen into creaking decrepitude; the cabins are without windows or doors—these having been taken to some newer hamlet; ridge-poles are sunken, chimneys tottering; soot covers the gaunt bones, which for all the world are like a row of skeletons, perched high, and grinning down at you in their misery; while the black offal of the pit, covering deep the original beauty of the once green slope, is in its turn being veiled with climbing weeds—such is Nature's haste, when untrammeled, to heal the scars wrought by man.

pp. 7–8

At six o'clock a camping-ground for the night became desirable. We were fortunate, last evening, to find a bit of rustic country in which to pitch our tent; but all through this afternoon both banks of the river were lined with village after village, city after city, scarcely a garden patch between them— Wilson, Coal Valley, Loststock, Glassport, Dravosburg, and a dozen others not recorded on our map, which bears date of 1882. . . . The broad mouth of the Youghiogheny . . . is implanted with a cluster of iron-mill towns, of which McKeesport is the center. So far as we could see down the Monongahela, the air was thick with the smoke of glowing chimneys, and the pulsating whang of steel-making plants and rolling-mills made the air tremble. The view up the "Yough" was more inviting; so, with oars and paddle firmly set, we turned off our course and lustily pulled against the strong current of the tributary. A score or two of house-boats lay tied to the McKeesport shore or were bolstered high upon the beach; a fleet of Yough steamers had their noses to the wharf; a half-dozen fishermen were setting nets; and, high over all, with lofty spans of iron cobweb, several railway and wagon bridges spanned the gliding stream.

pp. 13–14

May 6

Camp on the Youghiogheny
above McKeesport, Pennsylvania

May 6

Traveling junk-boat

McKeesport, Pennsylvania

There was a smart thunder-shower during breakfast, followed by a cool, cloudy morning. At eleven o'clock Pilgrim was laden. A southeastern breeze ruffled the waters of the Yough, and for the first time the Doctor ordered up the sail, with W—at the sheet. It was not long before Pilgrim had the water "singing at her prow." With a rush we flew past the factories, the house-boats, and the shabby street-ends of McKeesport, out into the Monongahela, where, luckily, the wind still held.

p. 16

The noisy iron-
manufacturing town of Braddock
now occupies the site of
Braddock's defeat. Not far from
the old ford stretches the great
dam of Lock No. 2, which we
portaged, with the usual difficul-
ties of steep, stony banks.

p. 17

(X3)49427

May 6

Dam at Lock No. 2

Braddock, Pennsylvania

May 6

Edgar W. Thomson steel works

on the Monongahela

Braddock, Pennsylvania

*B*raddock is but eight
miles across country from
Pittsburg, although twelve by
river. We have, all the way down,
an almost constant succession of
iron and steel-making towns,
chief among them Homestead,
on the left bank, seven miles
above Pittsburg.

p. 17

(X3)49428

May 6

Three boys in crude boat
on the Monongahela
below Braddock, Pennsylvania

May 6

Ferry with Sunday passengers
on the Monongahela
below Homestead, Pennsylvania

To-day, the Homesteaders are enjoying their Sunday afternoon outing along the town shore—nurses pushing baby carriages, self-absorbed lovers holding hands upon riverside benches, merry-makers rowing in skiffs or crossing the river in crowded ferries; the electric cars, following either side of the stream as far down as Pittsburg, crowded to suffocation with gayly-attired folk. They look little like rioters; yet it seems but the other day when Homestead men and women and children were hysterically reveling in atrocities akin to those of the Paris commune.

p. 18

The names they bear interest us, as betokening, perhaps, the proclivities of their owners. "Little Joe," "Little Jim," "Little Maggie," and like diminutives, are common here, as upon the towing-tugs and steam ferries of broader waters—and now and then we have, by contrast, "Xerxes," "Achilles," "Hercules." Sometimes the skiff is named after its owner's wife or sweetheart, as "Maggie G.," "Polly H.," or from the rustic goddesses, "Pomona," "Flora," "Ceres;" on the Kentucky shore, we have noted "Stonewall Jackson," and "Robert E. Lee," and one Ohio boat was labeled "Little Phil." Literature we found represented to-day, by "Octave Thanet"—the only case on record, for the Ohio-River "cracker" is not greatly given to books. Slang claims for its own, many of these knockabout craft— "U. Bet," "Git Thair," "Go it, Eli," "Whoa, Emma!" and nondescripts, like "Two Doves," "Poker Chip," and "Game Chicken," are not infrequent.

pp. 253–54

May 7

House boat "Two Doves"
on the Ohio River
near Beaver, Pennsylvania

May 8

Deserted cabin

10 miles below Beaver, Pennsylvania

assing Beaver River, the Ohio enters upon its grand sweep to the southwest. The wide uplands at once become more rustic, especially those of the left bank, which is no longer threaded by a railway, as heretofore all the way from Brownsville. The two ranges of undulating hills, some three hundred and fifty feet high, forming the rim of the basin, are about a half mile apart; while the river itself is perhaps a third of a mile in width, leaving narrow bottoms on alternate sides, as the stream in gentle curves rebounds from the rocky base of one hill to that of another. When winding about such a base, there is at this stage of the water a sloping, stony beach, some ten to twenty yards in width, from which ascends the sharp steep, for the most part heavily tree-clad—maples, birches, elms and oaks of goodly girth, the latter as yet in but half-leaf.

pp. 30–31

(X3)49433

On the "bottom side" of the river, the alluvial terrace presents a sheer wall of clay rising from eight to a dozen feet above the beach, which is often thick-grown with willows, whose roots hold the soil from becoming too easy a prey to the encroaching current. Sycamores now begin to appear in the bottoms, although of less size than we shall meet below. Sometimes the little towns we see occupy a narrow and more or less rocky bench upon the hillside of the stream, but settlement is chiefly found upon the bottoms.

p. 31

(X3)49435

May 8

Cultivated hillsides

near Industry, Pennsylvania

May 8

Man with nitroglycerin

Shippingport, Pennsylvania

ilgrim and her crew . . . were visited by a breezy, red-faced young man, in a blue flannel shirt and a black slouch hat. . . . He was a dealer in nitro-glycerin cartridges, he said, and pointed to a long, rakish-looking skiff hard by, which bore a red flag at its prow. "Ye see that? Thet there red flag? Well, thet's the law on us glyser*een* fellers— over five hundred poun's, two flags; un'er five hundred, one flag. I've two hundred and fifty, I have. I tell yer th' steamboats steer clear o' me, an' don' yer fergit it, nei-ther; they jist give me a wide berth, they do, yew bet! 'n' th' railroads, they don' carry no gly-ser*een* cartridge, they don't—all uv it by skiff, like yer see me goin'."

Wouldn't the Doctor go into partnership with him? He had no caps for his cartridges, and if the Doctor would buy caps and "stan' in with him on the cost of the glyser*een*," they would, regardless of Ohio statutes, blow up the fish in unfrequented por-tions of the river, and make two hundred dollars apiece by carry-ing the spoils in to Wheeling. The Doctor, as a law-abiding cit-izen, good-naturedly declined.

pp. 31–32, 33–34

By the middle of the afternoon we reached the boundary line . . . between Pennsylvania on the east and Ohio and West Virginia on the west. The last Pennsylvania settlements are a half mile above the boundary—Smith's Ferry . . . an old and somewhat decayed village, on a broad, low bottom at the mouth of the picturesque Little Beaver Creek; and Georgetown . . . a prosperous-looking sedate town, with tidy lawns running down the edge of the terrace, below which is a shelving stone beach of generous width. . . . Upon the left bank, surmounting a high, rock-strewn beach, is the dilapidated frame house of a West Virginia "cracker," through whose garden-patch the line takes its way, unobserved and unthought of by pigs, chickens, and children, which in hopeless promiscuity swarm the interstate premises.

pp. 34, 35

(X3)49437

May 8

House in W. Virginia

garden in Pennsylvania

May 9

W. Virginia bank

below New Cumberland

—'s enthusiasm for botany frequently takes us ashore. Landing at the foot of some eroded steep which, with ragged charm, rises sharply from the gravelly beach, we fasten Pilgrim's painter to a stone, and go scrambling over the hillside in search of flowers. . . . The view from projecting rocks, in these lofty places, is ever inspiring; the country spread out below us, as in a relief map; the great glistening river winding through its hilly trough; a rumpled country for a few miles on either side, gradually trending into broad plains, checkered with fields on which farmsteads and rustic villages are the chessmen.

pp. 42–43

(X3)49438

ilgrim is indeed a curiosity hereabout. What remarks we overhear are about her, — "Honey skiff, that!" "Right smart skiff!" "Good skiff for her place, but no good for this yere river!" and so on. She is a lapstreak, square-sterned craft, of white cedar three-eighths of an inch thick; fifteen feet in length and four of beam; weighs just a hundred pounds; comfortably holds us and our luggage, with plenty of spare room to move about in; is easily propelled, and as staunch as can be made. Upon these waters, we meet nothing like her.

p. 51

(X3)49439

May 9

Reuben aboard the Pilgrim
below New Cumberland, W. Virginia

May 10

Friends seeing us off

Mingo Junction, Ohio

hree miles below Steubenville is Mingo Junction, where we are the guests of a friend who is superintendent of the iron and steel works here. . . . A visit to a great steel-making plant, in full operation, is an event in a man's life. Particularly remarkable is the weird spectacle presented at night, with the furnaces fiercely gleaming, the fresh ingots smoking hot, the Bessemer converter "blowing off," the great cranes moving about like things of life, bearing giant kettles of molten steel; and amidst it all, human life held so cheaply. Nearer to medieval notions of hell comes this fiery scene than anything imagined by Dante. The working life of one of these men is not over ten years, B— [Superintendent William H. Bradley] says. A decade of this intense heat, compared to which a breath of outdoor air in the close mill-yard, with the midsummer sun in the nineties, seems chilly, wears a man out— "only fit for the boneyard then, sir," was the laconic estimate of an intelligent boss whom I questioned on the subject.

pp. 44, 45

There are, in the course of the summer, so many sorts of people traveling by the river, — steamboat passengers, campers, fishers, houseboat folk, and what not. . . . The regulation Ohio river skiff is built on graceful lines, but of inch boards, heavily ribbed, and is a sorry weight to handle. The contention is, that to withstand the swash of steamboat wakes breaking upon the shore, and the rush of drift in times of flood, a heavy skiff is necessary.

pp. 50–51

(X3)49441

May 10

Fishermen 4 miles above
Wheeling, W. Virginia

50

May 10

Outskirts

Wheeling, W. Virginia

The houseboats, dozens of which we see daily, interest us greatly. They are scows, or "flats," greatly differing in size, with low-ceilinged cabins built upon them—sometimes of one room, sometimes of half a dozen, and varying in character from a mere shanty to a well-appointed cottage. Perhaps the greater number of these craft are afloat in the river, and moored to the bank, with a gang-plank running to shore; others are "beached," having found a comfortable nook in some higher stage of water, and been fastened there, propped level with timbers and driftwood.... A goodly proportion of these boats are inhabited by the lowest class of the population, —poor "crackers" who have managed to scrape together enough money to buy, or enough energy and driftwood to build, such a craft; and, near or at the towns, many are occupied by gamblers, illicit liquor dealers, and others who, while plying nefarious trades, make a pretense of following the occupation of the Apostles.

pp. 52, 53

Wheeling had become the
western end of a wagon road
across the Panhandle, from
Redstone [Brownsville], and here
were fitted out many flatboat
expeditions for the lower Ohio;
later, in steamboat days, the shal-
low water of the upper river
caused Wheeling to be in midsummer the highest port attainable; and to this day it holds its
ground as the upper terminus of
several steamboat lines.

pp. 61–62

May 10

Ferry

Wheeling, W. Virginia

May 10

Wharf

Wheeling, W. Virginia

By the middle of the afternoon, we were at Wheeling. The town has fifty thousand inhabitants, is substantially built, of a distinctly Southern aspect; well stretched out along the river, but narrow; with gaunt, treeless, gully-washed hills of clay rising abruptly behind, giving the place a most forbidding appearance from the water. There are several fine bridges spanning the Ohio; and Wheeling Creek, which empties on the lower edge of town, is crossed by a maze of steel spans and stone arches; the well-paved wharf, sloping upward from the Ohio, is nearly as broad and imposing as that of Pittsburg.

p. 59

The chief feature of the place is the great Indian mound—the "Big Grave of early chroniclers." This earthwork is one of the largest now remaining in the United States, being sixty-eight feet high and a hundred in diameter at the base, and has for over a century attracted the attention of travelers and archaeologists.

We found it at the end of a straggling street on the edge of the town, a quarter of a mile back from the river. Around the mound has been left a narrow path of ground, utilized as a corn field; and the stout picket fence which encloses it bears peremptory notice that admission is forbidden. However, as the proprietor was not easily accessible, we exercised the privilege of historical pilgrims, and letting ourselves in through the gate, picked our way through rows of corn, and ascended the great core.

pp. 64–65

May 11

South side of Indian mound

Moundsville, W. Virginia

May 11

East side of Indian mound

Moundsville, W. Virginia

It is covered with a heavy growth of white oaks, some of them three feet in diameter, among which the path picturesquely zigzags. The summit is fifty-five feet in diameter, and the center somewhat depressed, like a basin. From the middle of this basin a shaft some twenty-five feet in diameter has been sunk by explorers, for a distance of perhaps fifty feet; at one time, a level tunnel connected the bottom of this shaft with the side of the cone, but it has been mostly obliterated. A score of years ago, tunnel and shaft were utilized as the leading attractions of a beer garden—to such base uses may a great historical landmark descend!

pp. 65–66

May 11

Here, late in October or early in November, 1772, young George Rogers Clark made his first stake west of the Alleghanies, rudely cultivating a few acres of forest land on what is now called Cresap's Bottom, surveying for the neighbors, and in the evenings teaching their children in the little log cabin of his friend, Yates Conwell, at the mouth of Fish Creek, a few miles below.

p. 72

Cresap's Bottom, W. Virginia
looking toward Ohio shore

May 12

Oil wells

Witten's Bottom, Ohio

All about us were the ugly, towering derricks of oil and natural gas wells—Witten's Bottom on the right, with its abutting hills; the West Virginia woods across the river, and the maple-strewn island between, all covered with scaffolds. The country looks like a rumpled fox-and-geese board, with pegs stuck all over it. A mile and a half below lies Sistersville, W. Va., the emporium of this greasy neighborhood—great red oil-tanks and smoky refineries its chiefest glory; crude and raw, like the product it handles.

Oil was "struck" here two or three years ago, and now within a distance of a few miles there are hundreds of wells— "two hun'rd in this yere gravel alone, sir!" I was told by a red-headed man in a red shirt, who lived with his numerous family in a twelve-foot-square box at the rear of a pumping engine.

It is a bewildering scene, with all these derricks thickly scattered around, engines noisily puffing, walking-beams forever rearing and plunging, the country cob-webbed with tumbling-rods and pipe lines, the shanties of the operatives with their rude lamp-posts, and the face of Nature so besmeared with the crude output of the wells that every twig and leaf is thick with grease.

pp. 78–79

The operatives dwell in little shanties scattered conveniently
about; in front of each is a vertical half-inch pipe, six or eight
feet high, bearing a half bushel of
natural-gas flame which burns
and tosses night and day, winter
and summer, making the Bottom
a warm corner of the earth,
when the unassisted temperature
is in the eighties.

p. 79

(X3)49450

May 12

Operator's shanty

Witten's Bottom, Ohio

58

May 12

Boys seeing us off
New Matamoras, Ohio

e were in several small towns to-day, in pursuance of the policy of distributing our shopping, so as to see as much of the shore life as practicable. Chief among them have been New Matamoras and St. Mary's in West Virginia, and Newport, in Ohio. Rather dingy villages, these— each, after their kind, with a stone wharf thick-grown with weeds; a flouring mill at the head of the landing; a few cheap-looking, battlemented stores; boys and men lounging about with that air of comfortable idling which impresses one as the main characteristic of rustic hamlets, where nobody seems ever to have anything to do; a ferry running to the opposite shore—for cattle and wagons, a heavy flat, with railings, made to drift with the current; and for foot passengers, a lumbering skiff, with oars chucking noisily in their roomy locks.

pp. 81–82

New Matamoras is in Ohio. Across the river is Matamoras, West Virginia.

Just above Witten's commences the Long Reach of the Ohio—a charming panorama, for sixteen and a half miles in a nearly straight line to the southwest.

p. 79

(X3)49452

Woman rowing

Long Reach of the Ohio

May 12

Mouth of Davis's Run

above St. Mary's, W. Virginia

ittle towns line the alternating bottoms, and farm-steads are numerous on the slopes. But they are rocky and narrow, these gentle shoulders of the hills, and a poor class of folk occupy them—half fishers, half farmers, a cross between my Round Bottom friend and the houseboat nomads.

pp. 79–80

(X3)49453

61

A picturesquely-dilapidated log house, with whitewashed porch in front, and a vine arbor at the rear, attracted our attention at the foot of the reach, near Grape Island. I clambered up, to photograph it. The ice was broken by asking for a drink of water. A gaunt girl of eighteen, the elder of two, with bare feet, her snaky hair streaming unkempt about a smirking face, went with a broken-nosed pitcher to a run, which could be heard splashing over its rocky bed near by. The meanwhile, I took a seat in the customary arcade between the living room and kitchen, and talked with her fat, greasy, red-nosed father, who confided to me that he was "a pi'neer from way back." He occupied his own land—a rare circumstance among these riverside "crackers;" had a hundred and thirty acres, worth twenty dollars the acre; "jist yon ways," back of the house, in the cliffside, there was a coal vein two feet thick, as yet only "worked" for his own fuel; and lately, he had struck a bank of firebrick clay which might some day be a "good thing for th' gals."

pp. 80–81

May 12

Log house

opposite Grape Island

May 12

Ohio family in log house

opposite Grape Island

On leaving, I casually mentioned my desire to photograph the family on the porch, where the light was good. While I walked around the house outside, they passed through the front room, which seemed to be the common dormitory as well as parlor. To my surprise and chagrin, the girls and their dowdy mother had, in those brief moments of transition, contrived to arrange their hair and dress to a degree which took from them all those picturesque qualities with which they had been invested at the time of my arrival. The father was being reproved, as he emerged upon the porch, for not "slick'n his ha'r, and wash'n' and fix'n' up, afore hav'n' his pictur' taken;" but the old fellow was obdurate, and joined me in remonstrance against this transformation to the commonplace, on the part of his women-folk. However, there was no profit in arguing with them, and I took my snap-shot with a conviction that the film was being wasted.

p. 81

(X3)49454

Our camp, to-night, is on a bit of grassy ledge at the summit of a rocky bank, ten miles above Marietta, on the Ohio side.... We had not yet pitched tent ... when our first camp-bore appeared—a middling-sized man, florid as to complexion, with a mustache and goatee, and in a suit of seedy black, surmounted by a crushed-in Derby hat.... I have seldom met a fellow with better staying qualities.... Patiently did he watch the prepa-ration of dinner, and spice each dish with commendations of W—'s skill at making the most of her few utensils.... He would take no bite with us, but sat and talked and talked, despite plain hints, growing plainer with the progress of time, that his family needed him at nightfall. Dinner was eaten and dishes washed; the others left on a botanical roundup, and I produced my writing materials, with remarks upon the lateness of the hour. At last our guest arose, shook the grass from his clothes, ... and as politely as possible expressed the great pleasure which the visit had given him.

pp. 82–84

(X3)49456

May 12

W. Virginia shore

seen from log house

May 12

Steamboat pushing coal barges

near Grape Island

The steamboat traffic is improving as we get lower down. Last evening, between landing and bedtime, a half dozen passed us, up and down, breathing heavily as dragons might, and leaving behind them foamy wakes which loudly broke upon the shore. Before morning, I was at intervals awakened by as many more. A striking spectacle, the passage of a big river steamer in the night; you hear, fast approaching, a labored pant; suddenly, around the bend, or emerging from behind an island, the long white monster glides into view, lanterns gleaming on two lines of deck, her electric searchlight uneasily flitting to and fro, first on one landmark, then on another, her engine bell sharply clanging, the measured pant developing into a burly, all-pervading roar, which gradually declines into a pant again—and then she disappears as she came, her swelling wake rudely ruffling the moonlit stream.

p. 88

(X3)49457

According to steamboat enthusiasts Jack and Sandra Custer, editors and publishers of *The Egregious Steamboat Journal,* this is the only known photograph of the *Clifton.*

The day broke without fog, at our camp on the rocky steep above Marietta. The eastern sky was veiled with summer clouds, all gayly flushed by the rising sun, and in the serene silence of the morning there hung the scent of dew, and earth, and trees.

In the east, the distant edges of the West Virginia hills were aglow with the mounting light before it had yet peeped over into the river trough, where a silvery haze lent peculiar charm to flood and bank. Up river, one of the Three Brothers isles, dark and heavily forested, seemed in the middle ground to float on air. A bewitching picture this, until at last the sun sprang clear and strong above the fringing hills, and the spell was broken.

p. 87

(X3)49458

May 13

Jessie wiping dishes

above Marietta, Ohio

May 13

Merchant boat

above Marietta, Ohio

went down shore a hundred yards, struggling through the dense fringe of willows, to photograph a junk-boat just putting off into the stream. The two rough-bearded, merry-eyed fellows at the sweeps were setting their craft broadside to the stream—that "the current might have more holt of her," the chief explained. They were interested in the kodak, and readily posed as I wished, but wanted to see what had been taken, having the common notion that it is like a tintype camera, with results at once attainable.

pp. 89–90

"The first thing that strikes a stranger from the Atlantic," says Flint (1814), "is the singular, whimsical, and amusing spectacle of the varieties of water-craft, of all shapes and structures."

p. 162

(X3)49460

Thwaites is quoting from Timothy Flint, *Recollection of the Last Ten Years* (Boston, 1826).

May 14

Big man in little boat

below Parkersburg, W. Virginia

May 15

Log house against cliff

Long Bottom, Ohio

e stopped just below camp, at an especially picturesque Ohio hamlet, —Long Bottom, —where the dozen or so cottages are built close against the bald rock.... One sprawling log house, fairly embowered in vines, and overtopped by the palisade rising sheer for thirty feet above its back door, looked in this setting for all the world like an Alpine chalet, lacking only stones on the roof to complete the picture. I took a kodak shot at this.
pp. 109, 110

(X3)49462

I took a kodak . . . also at a group of tousle-headed children at the door of a decrepit shanty built entirely within a crevice of the rock—their Hibernian mother, with one hand holding an apron over her head, and the other shielding her eyes, shrilly crying to a neighboring cliff-dweller: "Miss McCarthy! Miss McCarthy! There's a feller here a photegraph'n' all the people in the Bottom! Come, quick!" Then they eagerly pressed around me, Germans and Irish, big and little, women and children mostly, asking for a view of the picture, which I gave all in turn by letting them peep into the ground-glass "finder"—a pretty picture, they said it was, with the colors all in, and "wonderfully like," though a wee bit small.

Speaking of color, we are daily struck with the brilliant hues in the workaday dresses of women and children seen along the river. Red calico predominates, but blues and yellows, and even greens, are seen, brightly splashing the somber landscape.

pp. 110–11

(X3)49461

May 15

Children at cliff dwelling

Long Bottom, Ohio

May 24

Vanishing view

Cincinnati, Ohio

No doubt we all breathed freer when Pilgrim, too, was beached, —although it be only confessed in the privacy of the log. With her and her cargo safely stored in the wharf-boat, we sought a hotel, and, regaining our bag of clothing, —shipped ahead of us from McKee's Rocks, —donned urban attire for an inspection of the city. And a noble city it is.

p. 178

A strong head wind, meeting this surging tide, is lashing it into a white-capped fury. But lying to with paddle and oars, and dodging ferries and towing-tugs as best we may, Pilgrim bears us swiftly past the long line of steamers at the wharf, past Newport and Covington, and the insignificant Licking, and out under great railway bridges which cobweb the sky. Soon Cincinnati, shrouded in smoke, has disappeared around the bend, and we are in the fast-thinning suburbs—homes of beer-gardens and excursion barges, havens for freight-flats, and villas of low and high degree.

p. 183

May 26

Ferry between

Rabbit Hash, Kentucky,

and Rising Sun, Indiana

May 26

Ferry and ferryman

Rabbit Hash, Kentucky

I tried to ascertain the origin of the name Rabbit Hash, as applied to the hamlet. Every one had a different opinion, evidently invented on the spur of the moment, but all "'lowed" that none but the tobacco agent could tell, and he was off in the country for the day; as for themselves, they had, they confessed, never thought of it before. It always had been Rabbit Hash, and like enough would be to the end of time.

p. 191

(X3)49465

There is a small general
store in Rabbit Hash, with
postoffice and paint-shop attach-
ment, and near by a tobacco
warehouse and a blacksmith
shop, with a few cottages scattered at intervals over the bottom. The postmaster, who is
also the storekeeper and painter,
greeted me with joy, as I depos-
ited with him mail-matter bearing eighteen cents' worth of
stamps; for his is one of those
offices where the salary is the
value of the stamps cancelled.
It is not every day that so liberal
a patron comes along.

pp. 189–90

(X3)49466

May 26

General Store

Rabbit Hash, Kentucky

May 26

Palisades

on Big Bone Creek, Kentucky

ig Bone Creek, some fifty or sixty feet wide at the mouth, opens through a willow patch, between pretty, sloping hills. A houseboat lay just within—a favorite situation for them, these creek mouths, for here they are undisturbed by steamer wakes, and the fishing is usually good. The prop[r]ietor, a rather distinguished-looking mulatto, despite his old clothes and plantation straw hat, was sitting in a chair at his cabin door, angling; his white wife was leaning over him lovingly, as we shot into the scene, but at once withdrew inside. This man, with his side-whiskers and fine air, may have been a headwaiter or a dance-fiddler in better days; but his soft, plaintive voice, and hacking cough, bespoke the invalid. He told us what he knew about the creek, which was little enough, as he had but recently come to these parts.

pp. 192-93

The source of Big Bone Creek is a marshy basin some fifty acres in extent, rimmed with gently-sloping hills, and freely pitted with copious springs of a water strongly sulphurous in taste, with a suggestion of salt. The odor is so powerful as to be all-pervading, a quarter of a mile away, and to be readily detected at twice that distance. This collection of springs constitutes Big Bone Lick, probably the most famous of the many similar licks in Kentucky, Indiana, and Illinois.

This one was first visited by the French as early as 1729, and became famous because of the great quantities of remains of animals which lay all over the marsh, particularly noticeable being the gigantic bones of the extinct mammoth—hence the name adopted by the earliest American hunters, "Big Bone." Pioneer chronicles abound in references to the Lick, and we read frequently of hunting parties using the ribs of the mammoth for tent poles, and sections of the vertebrae as camp stools and tables. But in our own day, there are no surface evidences of this once rich treasure of giant fossils.
pp. 197–98

May 26

William and Fred

Big Bone Lick, Kentucky

May 27

Farm boys watering horses

Vevay, Indiana

Vevay . . . a small town on a low-lying bottom, is neat and apparently prosperous. Vevay was settled in 1803, by John James Dufour and several associates, from the District of Vevay, in Switzerland, who purchased from Congress four square miles hereabout, and, christening it New Switzerland, sought to establish extensive vineyards in the heart of this middle West. The Swiss prospered. The colony has had sufficient vitality to preserve many of its original characteristics unto the present day.

Much of the land in the neighborhood is still owned by the descendants of Dufour and his fellows, but the vineyards are not much in evidence. In fact, the grape-growing industry on the banks of the Ohio, although commenced at different points with great promise, by French, Swiss, Germans, and Americans alike, has not realized their expectations. The Ohio has proved to be unlike the Rhine in this respect. In the long run, the vine in America appears to fare better in a more northern latitude.

pp. 204–5

(X3)49469

The introduction of steamboats (1814) soon effected a revolution. A steamer could carry ten times as much as a barge, could go five times as fast, and required fewer men; it traveled at night, quickly passing from one port to another, pausing only to discharge or receive cargo; its owners and officers were men of character and responsibility, with much wealth in their charge, and insisted on discipline and correct deportment. The flatboat and the keelboat were soon laid up to rot on the banks; and the boatmen either became respectable steamboat hands and farmers, or went into the Far West, where wild life was still possible

pp. 165–66

(X3)49470

May 27

Steamer "Sunshine"
near Vevay, Indiana

May 27

Junk boat "Ivory Wood No. 3"
Indian Kentucky River

𝓘nterspersed with the houseboat folk, although of different character, are those whose business leads them to dwell as nomads upon the river—merchant peddlers, who spend a day or two at some rustic landing, while scouring the neighborhood for oil-barrels and junk, which they load in great heaps upon the flat roofs of their cabins, giving therefor, at goodly prices, groceries, crockery, and notions, — often bartering their wares for eggs and dairy products, to be disposed of to passing steamers, whose clerks in turn "pack" them for the largest market on their route.

p. 55

The Indian Kentucky, a small stream but half-a-dozen rods wide, enters from the north, five miles below— "Injun Kaintuck," it was called by a jovial junk-boat man stationed at the mouth of the tributary. There are, on the Ohio, several examples of this peculiar nomenclature: a river enters from the south, and another affluent coming in from the north, nearly opposite, will have the same name with the prefix "Indian." The reason is obvious; the land north of the Ohio remained Indian territory many years after Kentucky and Virginia were recognized as white man's country, hence the convenient distinction—the river coming in from the north, near the Kentucky, for instance, became "Indian Kentucky," and so on through the list.

pp. 206–7

(X3)49472

May 27

Crowd seeing us off

Indian Kentucky River

May 29

Crowd seeing us off

wharf at Louisville, Kentucky

Noises, far different from the clash of savage arms, are in the air to-night. Far above our heads a great iron bridge crosses the Ohio, some of its piers resting on the island, —a busy combination thoroughfare for steam and electric railways, for pedestrians and for vehicles, plying between New Albany and Portland. The whirr of the trolley, the scream and rumble of locomotives, the rattle of wagons; and just above the island head, the burly roar of steamboats signaling the locks, —these are the sounds which are prevalent. Through all this hubbub, electric lamps are flashing, and just now a steamer's search-light swept our island shore, lingering for a moment upon the little camp, doubtless while the pilot satisfied his curiosity. Let us hope that savage warriors never o' nights walk the earth above their graves; for such scenes as this might well cause those whose bones lie here to doubt their senses.

pp. 221–22

(X3)49473

We have had stately, eroded hills, and broad, fertile bottoms, hemming us in all day, and marvelous ox-bows in the erratic stream. The hillsides are heavily wooded, sometimes the slopes coming straight down to the stony beach, without intervening terrace; where there are such terraces, they are narrow and rocky, and the homes of shanty-men.

In the midst of this world of shade, nestle the whitewashed cabins of the small tillers; but though they swarm with children, it is not often that the inhabitants appear by the riverside. We catch a glimpse of them when landing on our petty errands, we now and then see a houseboater at his nets, and in the villages a few lackadaisical folk are lounging by the wharf; but as a rule, in these closing days of our pilgrimage, we glide through what is almost a solitude. The imagination has not to go far afield, to rehabilitate the river as it appeared to the earliest voyagers

pp. 224–25, 227

May 30

Houseboat

below Louisville, Kentucky

June 2

Wharf boat

Cloverport, Kentucky

loverport is a typical Kentucky town, of somewhat less than four thousand inhabitants. The wharf-boat, which runs up and down an iron tramway, according to the height of the flood, was swarming with negroes, watching with keen delight the departure of the "E. D. Rogan," as she noisily backed out into the river and scattered the crowds with great showers of spray from her gigantic stern-wheel. It was a busy scene on board—negro roustabouts shipping the gang-plank, and singing in a low pitch an old-time plantation melody; stokers, stripped to the waist, shoveling coal into the gaping furnaces; chambermaids hanging the ship's linen out to dry; passengers crowded by the shore rail, on the main deck; the bustling mate shouting orders, apparently for the benefit of landsmen, for no one on board appeared to heed him; and high up, in front of the pilot-house, the spruce captain, in gold-laced cap, and glass in hand, as immovable as the Sphinx.

pp. 240–41

At the head of the slope were a picturesque medley of colored folk, of true Southern plantation types, so seldom seen north of Dixie. Two wee picaninnies, drawn in an express cart by a half-dozen other sable elfs, attracted our attention, as W— and I went up-town for our day's marketing. We stopped to take a snap-shot at them, to the intense satisfaction of the little kink-haired mother of the twins, who, barring her blue calico gown, looked as if she might have stepped out of a Zulu group.

p. 241

(X3)49477

Children

Cloverport, Kentucky

June 2

Stone quarry

7 miles below Cloverport, Kentucky

In this district, coal-mines again appear, with their riverside tipples, and their offal defiling the banks. In general, these reaches have many of the aspects of the Monongahela, although the hills are lower, and mining is on a smaller scale. . . . Hereafter, to the mouth, we shall for the most part row between parallel walls of clay, with here and there a bank-side ledge of rock and shale, and now and then a cragged spur running out to meet the river. We have now entered the great corn and tobacco belt of the Lower Ohio, the region of annual overflow, where the towns seek the highlands, and the bottom farmers erect their few crude buildings on posts, prepared in case of exceptional flood to take to boats.

pp. 242, 243

The prevalent eagerness on the part of farmers to obtain the utmost from their land made it difficult, this evening, to find a proper camping-place. We finally found a narrow triangle of clay terrace, in Indiana, at the mouth of Crooked Creek, where not long since had tarried a house-boater engaged in making rustic furniture.

In blissful content we sit upon the bank, and drink in the glories of the night. The days of our pilgrimage are nearing their end, but our enthusiasm for this *al fresco* life is in no measure abating. That we might ever thus dream and drift upon the river of life, far from the labored strivings of the world, is our secret wish, tonight.

We had long been sitting thus, having silent communion with our thoughts, when the Boy, his little head resting on W—'s shoulder, broke the spell by murmuring from the fullness of his heart, "Mother, why cannot we keep on doing this, always?"

pp. 243–44, 245

(X3)49479

June 3

Camp at Crooked Creek, Indiana,
above Lewisport, Kentucky

June 3

Stern-wheel skiff

above Grandview, Indiana

This morning, we passed the Indiana hamlets of Lewisport and Grand View, and by noon were at Rockport, a smart little city of three thousand souls, romantically perched upon a great rock, which on the right bank rises abruptly from the wide expanse of bottom.

Frequently had we seen skiffs upon the shore, arranged with the stern paddle-wheels, turned by levers operated by men standing or sitting in the boat. But we had seen none in operation until, shooting down this side channel, we met such a craft coming up, manned by two fellows, who seemed to be having a treadmill task of it; they assured us, however, that when a man was used to manipulating the levers he found it easier than rowing, especially in ascending stream.

pp. 246–48

We are in a noisy corner of the world. Over on the Indiana bottom, a squeaky fiddle is grinding out dance-tunes, hymns, and ballads with charming indifference. We thought we detected in a high-pitched "Annie Laurie" the voice of the ferryman's daughter. There seems, too, to be a deal of rowing on the river, evidently Owensboro folk getting back to town from a day in the country, and country folk hieing home after a day in the city. The ferryman is in much demand, judging from the frequent ringing of his bell, —one on either bank, set between two tall posts, with a rope dangling from the arm. At early dusk, the cracked bell of the Owensboro Bethel resounded harshily in our ears, as it advertised an evening service for the floating population; and now the wheezy strains of a melodeon tell us that, although we stayed away, doubtless others have been attracted thither.

pp. 249–50

(X3)49482

June 4

Bethel, a church boat

Owensboro, Kentucky

June 4

Dredging fleet

5 miles above Scuffletown, Kentucky

Near the pretty group of French Islands, two government dredges, with their boarding barges, were moored to the Kentucky shore—waiting for coal, we were told, before resuming operations in the planting of a dike. I took a snap-shot at the fleet, and heard one man shout to another, "Bill, did yer notice they've a photograph gallery aboord?" They appear to be a jolly lot, these dredgers, and inclined to take life easily, in accordance with the traditions of government employ.

p. 253

(X3)49483

June 4

Logging

15 miles above Evansville, Indiana

June 4

Fishermen

Cypress Creek, Indiana

I wonder if a fisherman could, if he tried, be exact in his statements. One of them . . . declared that at this stage of the water he made forty and fifty dollars a week, "'n' I rek'n I ote to be contint." A few miles farther on, another complained that when the river was falling, the water was so muddy the fish would not bite. . . . The other day, when the river was rising, a Cincinnati follower of the apostle's calling averred that there was no use fishing when the water was coming up. As the variable Ohio is like the ocean tide, ever rising and falling, it would seem that the thousands in this valley who make fishing their livelihood must be playing a losing game.

pp. 251–52

(X3)49485

Both in town and country, the riffraff of the houseboat element are in disfavor.... For the truth is, the majority of those who "live on the river," as the phrase goes, have the reputation of being pilferers; farmers tell sad tales of despoiled chicken-roosts and vegetable gardens. From fishing, shooting, collecting chance driftwood, and leading a desultory life along shore, like the wreckers of old they naturally fall into this thieving habit. Having neither rent nor taxes to pay, and for the most part not voting, and having no share in the political or social life of landsmen, they are in the State, yet not of it, — a class unto themselves.

We have struck up acquaintance with many of them, and they are not bad fellows, as the world goes. Philosophers all, and loquacious to a degree. But they cannot, for the life of them, fathom the mystery of our cruise. We are not in trade? we are not fishing? we are not canvassers? we are not show-people? "What 'n' tarnation air ye, anny way? Oh come now! No fellers is do'n' th' river fur fun, that's sartin—ye're jist gov'm'nt agints! Thet's my way o' think'n'. Well, 'f ye kin find fun in't, then done go ahead, I say!"

pp. 54–55, 56

(X3)49486

92

June 4

Club boat
above Newburgh, Indiana

June 6

Indiana headland

near West Franklin

he rain, at first spasmodic, became at last persistent. . . . At Cypress Bend, twelve miles below Henderson, Kentucky, we ran into an Indiana hill, where on a steep slope of yellow shale, all strewn with rocks, our tent was hurriedly pitched. There was no driving of pegs into this stony base, so we weighted down the canvas with round-heads, and fastened our guys to bushes and boulders as best we might.

pp. 259-60

(X3)49487

*T*en miles below Henderson, was a little fleet of houseboats, lying in a thicket of willows along the Indiana beach. We stopped at one of them, and bought a small catfish for dinner. The fishermen seemed a happy company, in this isolated spot. The women were engaged in household work, but the men were spending the afternoon collected in the cabin of one of their number, who had recently arrived from Green River. While waiting for the fish to be caught in a live-box, I visited with the little band. . . . Huddled around the little stove, under the fly, the crew dined sumptuously *en course*, from canned soup down to strawberries for dessert, —for Evansville is a good market. It is not always, we pilgrims fare thus high—the resources of Rome, Thebes, Bethlehem, Herculaneum, and the other classic towns with which the Ohio's banks are dotted, being none of the best. Some days, we are fortunate to have aught in our larder.

pp. 259, 260

(X3)49488

June 6

Fishermen's net and live-box

West Franklin, Indiana

June 6

Trader's houseboat

above Mt. Vernon, Indiana

e met at intervals to-day, several houseboats, the most of them bearing the inscription prescribed by the new Kentucky license law, which is now being enforced, the essential features of which inscription are the home and name of the owner, and the date at which the license expires. The standard of education among houseboaters is evinced by the legend borne by a trader's craft which we boarded near Slim Island: "Lisens exp.rs Maye the 24 1895." The young woman in charge, a slender creature in a brilliant red calico gown, with blue ribbons at the corsage, had been but recently marrried to her lord, who was back in the country stirring up trade. She had few notions of business, and allowed us to put our own prices on such articles as we purchased. The stock was a curious medley—a few staple groceries, bacon and dried beef, candies, crockery, hardware, tobacco, a small line of patent medicines, in which blood-purifiers chiefly prevailed, bitters, ginger beer, and a glass case in which were displayed two or three women's straw hats, gaudily-trimmed. The woman said their custom was, to tie up to some convenient shore and "buy a little o' the farmers, 'n' in that way trade springs up," and thus become known. Two or three weeks would exhaust any neighborhood, whereupon they would move on for a dozen miles or so.

pp. 261–62

The feature of the day was the entrance, through a dreary stretch of clay banks, of the Wabash River, which divides Indiana from Illinois. Three hundred and sixty yards wide at the mouth, about half the width of the Ohio, it is the most important of the latter's northern affluents, and pours into the main stream a swift-rushing body of clear, green water, which at first boldly pushes over to the heavily-willowed Kentucky shore the roily mess of the Ohio, and for several miles exerts a considerable influence in clarification. The Lower Wabash, flowing through a soft clay bottom, runs an erratic course, and its mouth is a variable location, so that the bounds of Illinois and Indiana, hereabout, fluctuate east and west according to the exigencies of the floods.

p. 263

(X3)49490

June 6

Last view of Indiana
mouth of the Wabash River

June 7

Shanty boat

Shawneetown, Illinois

t a distance, Shawneetown appears as if built upon higher land than the neighboring bottom; but this proves, on approach, to be an optical illusion, for the town is walled in by a levee some thirty feet in height, above the top of which loom its chimneys and spires. Shawneetown, laid out in 1808, soon became an important post on the Lower Ohio, and indeed ranked with Kaskaskia as one of the principal Illinois towns, although in 1817 it still only contained from thirty to forty log dwellings. During the reign of the Ohio-River bargemen, it was notorious as the headquarters of the roughest elements in that boisterous class, and frequently the scene of most barbarous outrages— "the odious receptacle," says a chronicler of the time, "of filth and villany."

pp. 267–68

The farmers upon the wide bottoms of the lower reaches now invariably have their dwellings, corn-cribs, and tobacco-sheds set upon posts, varying from five to ten feet high, according to the surrounding elevation above the normal river level. . . . It is with something akin to awe that we look upon these buildings on stilts, for they bespeak, in times of great flood, a rise in the river of between fifty and sixty feet.

Three miles above Saline River, I scrambled up to photograph a farm-house of this character. In order to get the building within the field of the camera, it was necessary to mount a cob-house of loose rails, which did duty as a pig-pen. A young woman of eighteen or twenty years, attired in a dazzling-red calico gown, came out on the front balcony to see the operation; and, for a touch of life, I held her in talk until the picture was taken.

pp. 269–70

(X3)49493

June 7

Illinois farm house

above the Saline River

June 7

Father and children

mouth of the Saline River

Few of these small farmers own the lands they till; from Pittsburg down, the great majority of Ohio River planters are but tenants. The old families that once owned the soil are living in the neighboring towns, or in other parts of the country, and renting out their acres to these cultivators.

p. 271

(X3)49494

*U*sually the flooded bottoms are denuded of trees, save perhaps a narrow fringe along the bank, and a few dead trunks scattered here and there; while back, a third or a half-mile from the river, lies a dense line of forest, far beyond which rises the low rim of the basin. But just below Saline River, a lazy little stream of a few rods' width, the hills, now perhaps eighty or a hundred feet in height, again approach to the water's edge; and henceforth to the mouth we are to have alternating semi-circular, wooded bottoms and shaly, often palisaded uplands, grown to scrub and vines much in the fashion of some of the middle reaches.

A trading-boat was moored just within the Saline, where we stopped for lunch under a clump of sycamores. The owner obtains butter and eggs from the farmers, in exchange for his varied wares, and sells them at a goodly profit to passing steamers, which will always stop when flagged.

pp. 272–73

(X3)49495

June 7

Jessie and Fred

mouth of the Saline River

June 7

Cave in rock

Illinois

Approaching Cave-
in-Rock, Ill., the right bank is for
several miles an almost continu-
ous palisade of lime-stone, thick-
studded with black and brown
flints. In the breaking down of
this escarpment, popularly styled
Battery Rocks, numerous caves
have been formed, the largest of
which gave the place its name. It
is a rather low opening into the
rock, perhaps two hundred feet
deep, and the floor some twenty
feet above the present level of the
river; in times of flood, it is frequently so filled with water that
boats enter, and thousands of silly
people have, in two or three gen-
erations past, carved or painted
their names upon the vaulted
roof. . . . About 1801, a band of
robbers made these inner recesses
their home, and frequently sallied
thence to rob passing boats, and
incidentally to murder the crews.
pp. 273, 274

(X3)49496

St. Jacobs was a product of a
Baltimore, Maryland, patent
medicine company, which advertised extensively on rocks along
the river. The name also was
carried on the company's stern-
wheeler that was built in 1880.

*C*arrsville, Ky., is another arid, hillside hamlet, with striking escarpments stretching above and below for several miles. Mammoth boulders, a dozen or more feet in height, relics doubtless of once formidable cliffs, here line the riverside.

p. 276

A cracker and his wife, fishing at the base of one giant [boulder], would have made an excellent study in blue jeans, sky blue sun bonnet, gray suit of man and red calico of the woman—a bright picture and a photographed item.

(Notebook 3, 1-11 June 1894)

(X3)49497

June 8

Man and wife fishing
below Carrsville, Kentucky

June 10

Cows on beach

Illinois shore

The settlements are meager, and now wholly in Illinois: For instance, Joppa, a row of a half-dozen unpainted, dilapidated buildings, chiefly stores and abandoned warehouses, bespeaking a river traffic of the olden time, that has gone to decay; a hot, dreary, baking spot, this Joppa, as it lies sprawling upon the clay ridge, flanked by a low, wide gravel beach, on which gaunt, bell-ringing cows are wandering, eating the leaves of fallen trees, for lack of better pasturage
pp. 290–91

(X3)49499

The Fort Massac ridge
extends down stream as far as
Mound City, but soon degener-
ates into a ridge of clay varying
in height from twenty-five to
fifty feet above the water level.
Upon the low-lying bottom of
the Kentucky shore, is still an
interminable dark line of forest.

A fisherman comes occasionally into view, upon this wide
expanse of wood and water and
clay-banks; sometimes we hail
him in passing, always getting a
respectful answer, but a stare of
innocent curiosity.

pp. 290, 292

June 10

Clay bank

below Joppa, Illinois

June 11

Men unloading coal barge

Cairo, Illinois

Quickly passing Mound City, now bustling with life, Pilgrim closely skirted the monotonous clay-banks of Illinois, swept rapidly under the monster railway bridge which stalks high above the flood, and loses itself over the tree-tops of the Kentucky bottom, and at a quarter-past eight o'clock was pulled up at Cairo, with the Mississippi in plain sight over there, through the opening in the forest. In another hour or two, she will be housed in a box-car; and we, her crew, having again donned the garb of landsmen, will be speeding toward our northern home, this pilgrimage but a memory.

Such a memory! As we dropped below the Towhead, the Boy, for once silent, wistfully gazed astern. When at last Pilgrim had been hauled upon the railway levee, and the Doctor and I had gone to summon a shipping clerk, the lad looked pleadingly into W—'s face. In tones half-choked with tears, he expressed the sentiment of all: "Mother, is it really ended? Why can't we go back to Brownsville, and do it all over again?"

pp. 294–95

Designer: Dean Johnson Design, Inc., Indianapolis, Indiana

Typeface: Bembo

Typographer: GAC Shepard Poorman, Indianapolis, Indiana

Paper: 100 pound Signature Gloss White Text

Printer: GAC Shepard Poorman, Indianapolis, Indiana